Advance Praise

"Throughout life, we all encounter high and lows. When faced with adversity, we have a choice: to retreat or to confront challenges head-on like an IRONMAN. Alex Cooper embodies this spirit of resilience, forged not solely by his IRONMAN finishes but by his unwavering commitment to self-discovery. His journey epitomizes the belief that with determination and a positive mindset, Anything is Possible."
—Mike Reilly, Voice of IRONMAN, USA Triathlon Hall of Fame, and IRONMAN Hall of Fame

'Alex Cooper's entrepreneurial spirit is truly inspiring. I have seen firsthand how his relentless determination and unwavering drive can ignite hope in others. Through his coaching, mentoring, and help nurturing nascent entrepreneurs with the Founder Institute, Alex has demonstrated that anyone with the right mindset can embark on the journey of building something impactful.'
—Jonathan Greechan, Co-Founder & CEO of Founder Institute

"Alex's leadership at Bizware was instrumental in creating additional value for the Ross Systems product line. His team's ability to enhance their software and ensure that it worked seamlessly with our products was a true testament to his vision and collaborative spirit. The strong partnership we built under Alex's guidance was a significant contribution to the value of our company."
—Ken Ross, Chairman of MedaSystems, software industry entrepreneur and angel investor

"Alex Cooper's resolve and strength are undeniable examples of the best of the human spirit. His story is so much more than defiance in the face of devastation. It's about making each day, each moment, each breath count. For that, his tome is uplifting and inspirational"
—Howie Rose, National Jewish Sports Hall of Fame inductee, Emmy awards receiver for Excellence in Broadcasting for the New York Islanders, New York Baseball Hall of Fame, Mets Hall of Fame

'Alex Cooper is constantly challenging the status quo—forcing us to think differently and act accordingly. I met Alex early on in my entrepreneurial journey, and his wisdom helped me through some tumultuous times. This book is an opportunity to share his wisdom even more broadly. Alex's story shines as a beacon of hope and resilience through the shadows of illness. His powerful storytelling allows Alex to share his journey as a cancer survivor, reminding us all that even in our darkest moments, there is light, courage, and the possibility of a new beginning.'
—Edrizio De La Cruzis a Y Combinator visiting partner; co-founder of Arcus, a fintech company sold to Mastercard in its largest Latam acquisition ever.

"The Courage to Start What You'll Finish is a poignant narrative that beautifully encapsulates the resilience and courage of a cancer survivor. Through raw honesty and unwavering determination, Alex navigates the turbulent journey of diagnosis, treatment, and ultimately, triumph. This compelling memoir is not just a story of survival, but a testament to the power of hope, love, and the human spirit. A must-read for anyone seeking inspiration and insight into the indomitable strength of the human heart.
—Wole Coaxum, Founder & CEO, Mobility Capital Finance, Inc. ("MoCaFi")

The Courage to Finish What You Started
From Startups to Ironman to Fighting Cancer

By Alex Cooper

The Courage to Finish What You Started: From Startups to Ironman to Fighting Cancer
Tasfil Publishing LLC
New Jersey, USA
Copyright © 2024 Alex Cooper

All rights reserved, including the right of reproduction in whole or in part in any form.

The author of this book does not dispense medical advice or prescribe the use of any technique as a form of treatment for physical, emotional, or medical problems without the advice of a physician, either directly or indirectly. The intent of the author is only to offer information of a general nature to help you in your quest for emotional or spiritual well-being. In the event you use any of the information in this book for yourself, which is your constitutional right, the author and publisher assume no responsibility for your actions.

This book is a memoir. It reflects the contemporaneous recollections of the author's experiences over time. The conversations found here come from memories and are not written to represent word-for-word transcripts. The feeling and meaning of what was said, the essence of it, is completely accurate

Artwork by Nina Rosenberg Nemeth nina.nemeth@yahoo.com.

Ebook ISBN: 978-1964014197
Paperback ISBN-13: 978-1964014203

Library of Congress Control Number has been applied for.

This book is dedicated to my dear mother, Susan. Her valor, strength, grace, fortitude, and love have inspired me since birth.

To my soulmate and the love of my life, Beth: my wife and the spiritual inspiration of my life the last twenty years

And my two children, Evan and Jess.

Contents

The Starting Line 1

FIRST LEG: Diagnoses, Fate, and Beginnings 7

    Chapter 1: Live Life to Its Fullest 9

    Chapter 2: Keep Moving 21

    Chapter 3: Own the Narrative 35

    Chapter 4: I Am a Survivor 47

    Chapter 5: Starting From Scratch 63

SECOND LEG: Repairs, Recalibrations and Fortune 77

    Chapter 6: Stay in the Moment 79

    Chapter 7: "Shut Up, Legs" 89

    Chapter 8: Stand Your Ground 113

    Chapter 9: Be Consistent 125

    Chapter 10: How to Succeed—and Fail 143

THIRD LEG: Connections, Compassion, and a New Kind of Endurance 159

    Chapter 11: You Are an IRONMAN 161

    Chapter 12: Signs From Above 183

    Chapter 13: Not Done Yet 201

    Chapter 14: On Balance 217

Chapter 15: Core of the IronCEO	233
The "Big Finish"	241
Epilogue	245
About the Author	249

The Starting Line

I've always been partial to beginnings.

I started three technology companies from scratch. I've also competed in more than 80 races—running, cycling, and triathlons, including ten Ironman competitions. And while I'm proud to say I've finished every one of those races, I'll tell you this much: showing up to the starting line to take that initial plunge is the biggest challenge of all.

But this story, like all stories, must have an end.

That may seem like a foregone conclusion, but endings aren't always a given—at least, not the ones we planned. And while they can be bittersweet or scary or even tragic, endings can also bring great triumph and joy.

I have learned you can never take success or even the joy of starting something for granted. I know firsthand that not everyone who shows up to a race will cross the finish line.

Still, showing up in the first place? That matters more.

I'm not sure how or when the tumor in my brain started. Likely, while I trained for what—before it even started—already somehow felt like my final Ironman competition: the 2022 event in Madison, Wisconsin, held on the 21st anniversary of the September 11 attacks on New York City.

During that cold, windy, rain-soaked race, I remained blissfully unaware that my life would soon—suddenly—change forever.

At the time, I was the indomitable chief. The endurance executive. I like to go by "the IronCEO" when sharing my races with friends and followers—though most of the time, people just call me Alex.

It's been a few months since my diagnosis, and even as I begin writing these words, I don't know whether I'll race—let alone finish—another Ironman. But I can assure you that, while I'm still able, I will always commit to showing up in the first place and taking that initial plunge, in whatever I do.

This is my story. The ride of my life. My journey through discovering my survivor roots as the son of two Holocaust survivors growing up in Queens, New York, building my own fortune from the ground up—and then doing it again, without much in the way of help, guidance, or means.

It's a story of memory and movement, unspeakable losses, and finish-line smiles.

In these pages, I'll talk about what I call the IronCEO Mindset—and what happens to that mindset when endings try to close in too fast and too soon. I can't outrun a terminal cancer diagnosis, but I can keep putting one foot in front of the other. This is a book about showing up, always finding the fortitude to push through, and learning new ways to define both "endurance" and "survivor."

Looking back, it makes sense that I've always picked individual endurance sports like triathlons. I'm most comfortable and confident when I can rely on myself, without the need for teammates or coaches to tell me what to do.

Now, walking the solitary path of living with cancer, I feel called to connect—to not just reflect on but also share my journey.

Through all my travails and accomplishments, I learned my true mission in life: I wanted to use my experiences, acquired wisdom, and life stories to inspire others to overcome adversity; Whether it is a life-or-death struggle, dusting yourself off from a failure, or overcoming the fear of starting something new and daunting.

My story may not compare to the 9/11 heroes we honored that windy, rain-soaked day in Madison, but I believe I've picked up some nuggets of wisdom—and a few good stories too.

Triathlons remain solo endeavors, but for this ride, you're welcome to come along—if you think you can keep up and finish the race. But enough about endings; let's *get started*.

Ready?

Set...

Go!

FIRST LEG:
Diagnoses, Fate, and Beginnings

Chapter 1
Live Life to Its Fullest

September 11, 2022: Ironman Wisconsin

It was an unseasonably cold September day on the shores of Lake Monona in Madison, Wisconsin—where I stood, about to jump in for a pre-Ironman swim. First, I looked into a camera recording my "IronCEO" fundraiser video, and said the following:

"I'm unsure if I'll race another Ironman. I know that I will move forward, whatever I do with my life. We don't get to choose our destiny or what day we will have glory or sacrifice. Sometimes, our destiny chooses us."

I was sixty years old, but given my decades of triathlon training, I felt strong and confident. I'd certainly never considered retiring from triathlons before, so when those words came out, they surprised even me. Still, something told me new challenges lay ahead.

Just 17 weeks later, I was diagnosed with brain cancer.

I still recall the cold sweat I broke into while listening to the doctor's words—including one I'd never heard before:

"glioblastoma," a rare and fast-growing form of the disease. The doctor discussed my life expectancy in months, not years. I left the medical office numb and shaking.

Nothing had seemed amiss when I left my home base of Denver, Colorado, for Madison a few days before the 21st anniversary of 9/11. That year I was raising funds to honor fallen heroes through the Tunnel to Towers Foundation, founded in tribute to Stephen Siller, a New York firefighter who died in service that day. This cause hit home for me because, on the day the towers fell, claiming Siller's life and so many others, I was sitting in a West Street office, directly across from the World Trade Center.

I thought of that fateful day in New York as I dove into the water, and into what I somehow suspected to be my final triathlon. Little did I know then that this would be my last athletic event before taking on the unwilling mantle of "cancer patient."

It can feel lonely battling a disease—but since discovering cycling and endurance sports, I have become adept at solo endeavors. In a triathlon, once you hit the water, there's hardly any sound outside your breath and the soft splash as you take stroke after stroke. It's just you against the clock and yourself.

I always start at the back of my swim wave—meaning that I allow the faster swimmers to dive in first. Though I never fail to swim the distance, I do tend to move at the pace of a tortoise crossing the road, and I like to avoid getting kicked or swam over before I can find my rhythm.

Besides—as I told my wife, Beth, when she trained for her first triathlon—that moment after you first dive into frigid, open water, your body contracts and your breathing grows shallow. However, once I recalibrate to the cold and catch my breath, that first leg of the race actually quiets my mind and lowers my heart rate.

Over the course of the nearly two hours, it takes me to swim the first leg, I can get pretty deep inside my head, following thoughts to good and bad places. That day was no exception. As I swam, my thoughts returned to those words I'd just shared on camera about racing my last Ironman and moving ahead.

We don't get to choose our destiny or what day we will have glory or sacrifice. Sometimes, our destiny chooses us.

Those words were meant to generate positivity and growth. After all, in my public persona as the "IronCEO" competitor and fundraiser, I had developed a positive growth mindset—including a series of "IronCEO principles."

The first and foremost among those principles? That simple, but too often overlooked act of *living life to its absolute fullest—every single day*.

As the Roman Emperor and stoic philosopher Marcus Aurelius put it, "It is not death that a man should fear, but rather he should fear never beginning to live."

I had no idea how central Aurelius' advice—nor how prophetic my own words about destiny—were about to become.

First Signs

When you put your body through three months of grueling training, culminating in an epic race—a 2.4-mile swim, a 112-mile bike ride, and a 26.2-mile run—through sheets of rain and high winds...let's just say that settling back into a normal routine can take time.

I started my usual recovery with some easy 30-minute swims and walks to move the soreness and fatigue through my body. In the second week, I got back on the bike. Typically, though, physical recovery's a piece of cake...at least compared to the mental and emotional transition.

When a race like Ironman ends, it feels like standing in a room where someone's suddenly switched off the lights.

Without cheering crowds, event lighting, masses of co-competitors in wetsuits, and celebratory music pumped through loudspeakers at the finishing line—you're back to being a normal guy with a job, a family, and the mundane responsibilities of everyday life.

Like many triathletes, I'm drawn to extremes, thriving in those "glory and sacrifice" moments simulated by events like an Ironman. It's not as easy adjusting back to the anticlimax of the day-to-day.

In other words, it can feel easy to *live life to its fullest* while training and competing—or while launching and leading a company—compared to the quieter, gentler rhythms of my ordinary, post-race life.

But, more than usual, something felt amiss after that September race.

The first sign of trouble was my typing. Always a fast, accurate typist, I suddenly couldn't get through a sentence without multiple mistakes. I mixed up word order and jumbled sentence structure. It took ages to even send a text or write a short email, never mind a business proposal.

As this began impacting my work, I resorted to voice-to-text and found an online typing test to assess my skills. While I could type normally with my left hand, my right could barely find the keys. Not one to give up easily, I struggled through thirty minutes of mounting frustration before banging on the keyboard and slamming my laptop shut in a huff.

Not only that, but after a lifetime of long-distance cycling, I suddenly had trouble dismounting. This simple, familiar task—performed thousands of times without thought or effort—now required me to carefully, consciously orchestrate a series of surprising complex movements to untangle my legs from the bike frame.

Similarly, while skiing that late October, I noticed a strange sensation. When planting my right pole, I couldn't tell where it had landed relative to my body and skis. While I could still ski, the experience felt awkward and disorienting.

The most alarming moments came when driving—every now and then, while my foot still held down the brake pedal, my mind perceived it already hitting the gas.

I still hadn't considered the possibility of a serious, let alone terminal, illness. My God, I'd just completed an Ironman in high winds and constant, pouring rain. No major injury or illness had ever halted my training and racing, not once in over thirty years. Two weeks marked the longest I'd taken off to recover from minor dents and dings.

I knew I was getting older; in fact, I was literally a grandpa. My stepson, Ben, and his wife, Samantha, had welcomed their beautiful little girl named Noa, about two years earlier. In fact, right around the time I first began noticing my cancer symptoms, Beth and I got the happy news that her daughter, Molly, and son-in-law, Tomer, were expecting their first.

Still, I knew deep down that this was more than age slowing me down—and I wasn't fooling Beth, either. How could my basic coordination disappear overnight?

The bigger question, of course, was what to do next. My whole life has been a study of adaptation and resilience. I had to understand and overcome these challenges—somehow.

My first doctor's visit, with my internal medicine doctor, comprised simple neurological tests and the typical questions. Had I recently fallen or lost balance? Was I having trouble with my vision?

My answer was always no, per usual.

Most of the time, I didn't even bother reading medical questionnaires; I just went down the row checking "no." My resting heart rate sat below fifty. Before cancer, I'd never spent a single night in a hospital.

But there's always been one question I answered with a yes. That was, "Do you have any family medical history of cancer?"

I'm a big "yes" on that one.

Both of my parents died from cancer, young. My mother was just sixty-eight when she succumbed to the disease, and it took my father at only thirty-nine before I had a chance to know him. If I'm honest, I grew up expecting the same fate—but that didn't make it any easier to take.

Diagnosis

Initial blood tests and neurological tests came back inconclusive. When the doctor suggested I see a neurologist, I jumped into action, calling referrals from my doctor and several other practices. The best I got was an appointment with a nurse practitioner three *months* from now.

That was not going to cut it.

I needed a doctor I could trust with the proper expertise—and fast. After a few frantic calls, I remembered an old neurologist friend. Though I hadn't spoken to him in over thirty years, I called his office, made an appointment, and booked a flight from Denver to New Jersey in early December.

In a five-day window, we met three times for a comprehensive battery of brainwave and cognitive function tests. Also, inconclusive.

Among several possible explanations—including dementia and Alzheimer's—my neurologist friend mentioned the possibility of a tumor. But at that point, I shrugged it off. His final recommendation echoed that of the Denver physician.

I needed an MRI.

Let's be honest. I could have gotten that test within days, which would have been the logical choice given the circumstances. Instead, I found excuses to wait—at least until the first week of January, when I could apply the costs to my new insurance plan's deductible.

On Thursday, January 5, 2023, I entered the radiology clinic at 5 p.m. By 6 p.m., I was on my way to meet my daughter, Jess, for dinner at our favorite Lebanese restaurant. As the waiter served our baba ganoush and hummus sampler plate, I answered a call from the staff radiologist and asked her if we could speak tomorrow. With audible urgency in her voice, she requested that I call back later that same evening.

The news she gave shook me to my core.

Given my family's history of cancer, I should have expected this day, but I was sadly unprepared to receive it. The MRI pictures conclusively showed a tumor in my brain. The radiology center wanted me to return early the next morning for a more detailed MRI using a contrast medical dye.

Friday's test would display the same result: a lump the size of a clementine nestled in the left parietal lobe of my brain.

Denial and Acceptance

Few people know when they are going to die. Since I didn't want to be one of them, I wasn't particularly interested in this doctor's prognosis. Like I said before, I don't waste time comparing myself to others. Much like the stats of other triathletes, cancer survival rates are just numbers. Numbers about *other people*—and therefore none of my concern.

I only wanted to keep living—*today*, and every day after that—as fully as possible.

Overall, I have lived a charmed and beautiful life, but in the end, fate catches up to all of us. I've certainly had my share of obstacles and heartaches, too. I had narrowly escaped a personal disaster on 9/11, and during a sudden bicycle accident that killed my former girlfriend before my very eyes. Now, something (quite literally) buried deep in the back of my mind had moved front and center.

The reality of my diagnosis began sinking in, along with unfamiliar waves of uncertainty and fear. The knowledge that both of my parents, as well as aunts and cousins, all died from cancer now weighed on me. Normally so driven and self-assured, a new and very raw sense of vulnerability now seeped into my "IronCEO" armor.

Even before I shared my diagnosis, I would find myself staring a bit too long at my wife and children, thinking about this beautiful life and family I'd built. Like most things in life, I did it my way. Coincidentally, Beth and I both had two young kids, the exact same ages and genders—one 10-year-old girl and one 12-year-old boy each—from previous marriages when we met. Making this Brady Bunch family unit work always presented challenges, but I think we exceeded all expectations.

How would Beth and the kids react to this? How would our lives change after I shared the news? Could I find the strength and determination to maintain an optimistic outlook for my own sake—and for the ones I love?

In the days following my diagnosis I quickly—instinctively—turned all that fear, vulnerability, and sadness to a low simmer. I had to focus my mind on the present and direct all of my energy inward to my life force. For inspiration, I drew on my experience as an endurance athlete. If I had the determination and resilience to finish ten Ironmans, I knew I could battle my brain cancer.

Like it or not, we are who we believe we are. My mindset affirmed my belief that anything was possible. This mindset has led me to great achievements, including starting three successful companies and a lifelong passion for endurance sports.

When I signed up for my first Ironman race ten years before my diagnosis, I began a journey of self-exploration that would codify my life of physical and mental training into what I called the IronCEO mindset.

The lessons I learned from each Ironman competition helped me put into words my ideas about who I was and why I behaved as I did. Now I understand how mindset enabled me to overcome personal tragedies, found multiple tech startup companies, and endure a decade of Ironman races.

This cancer diagnosis would prove the ultimate test.

Fate and Fatalism

According to the neurosurgeon, my fast-growing tumor developed in only three or four months—a shockingly short time to discover you have incurable, terminal cancer. Could I have discovered the growth sooner? Would it have made a difference in my prognosis?

Knowing my family's medical history, I should have rushed myself to an imaging center for an MRI the instant my internal medicine doctor suggested it. Instead, I denied the most obvious possibility.

I wanted to chalk it up to normal cognitive decline as a sixty-year-old who's always been challenged in the memory department. My mother used to make me wear house keys on a shoelace around my neck so I wouldn't lose them. Even now, my children, wife, and close friends run a checklist when they're with me—

"Do you have your keys, wallet, phone?" It's not senility, but let's just say I'm absent-minded.

I searched for any way to rationalize my hope for an alternative diagnosis. Deep down, I dreaded the diagnosis, but until I heard a doctor say the words, "You have a brain tumor that is probably cancer," I could not face the reality of this inevitable outcome.

It was real now, and I couldn't escape it. But despite my initial hesitancy, I knew I had the strength and instincts to overcome the challenges ahead.

This same strength, these same instincts came through for me on 9/11, as I sat in my office in the World Financial Center in lower Manhattan—across the street from the 110-story World Trade Center. When the first plane hit, I saw flames shoot out of the southern side of the building. Without a view of impact, I had no idea what had happened.

My gut told me to run. I sprinted past the elevator and down thirty-nine flights of stairs to West Street—where I saw the upper floors of the World Trade Center engulfed in flames.

I reacted quickly and with urgency on that fateful day. At the time, I told myself these survival instincts helped me avoid the fate that faced over 2,000 people on 9/11. Later, I began to suspect that equal measures of luck and destiny determined my outcome that day.

There's a fine line between believing in fate and devolving into outright fatalism. It's likely that some combination of the two prevented me from moving faster once the specter of cancer appeared. I've always had a hunch that when it's your time, your actions may not matter.

As I told the cameras the day before September 11, 2022: "We don't get to choose our destiny or what day we will have glory or sacrifice."

It's natural to become fatalistic after enduring tragedy and trauma. Like me, television personalities Anderson Cooper and Stephen Cobert lost their parents at young ages. I've heard both celebrities say they never expected to live past the age of their deceased parents.

I can relate.

Genetics alone doesn't guarantee that history will repeat itself. Given my penchant for long bike rides and runs along roads, I could just as easily die in a car accident as from cancer. Still, one immutable fact remained: either due to the Holocaust or illness, neither my parents nor my grandparents lived into their golden years. This sobering knowledge may have contributed to my fatalistic outlook, but it also instilled in me the first principle of my IronCEO mindset: to live life to its fullest, every day.

Of course, it's easy for an IronCEO at the top of his game to live extreme moments of triumph, glory, or sacrifice 'to his fullest.' Launching—or selling—a company from the ground up. Crossing that finish line with arms raised and grin gleaming.

It's much harder to fully embody and appreciate all the post-race slump moments in between ordinary life...that is, until something like a cancer diagnosis wakes you up to the value and promise of every moment, no matter how familiar or mundane.

In some ways, my early denial was somewhat intentional—an admittedly misguided way of not wanting to let my destiny choose me. But though the January 8 diagnosis confirmed my worst fears, it also didn't change a damn thing.

I still chose to keep living—to battle this disease and live as long as possible.

We may not be able to know in advance how or when our stories end, but we can determine how we live these moments between birth and death—no matter how ordinary or how extreme. In this way, having the right mindset protects against fatalism and allows us to fully show up to each moment and give it our all.

Like Aurelius, I resolved to not let the fear of death hold me back from living each day to its fullest. As the child of survivors, I knew how much life could test one's resolve, and I knew the immense value of each moment, each breath—in spite of—or perhaps even because of, those tests.

I couldn't cheat death.

So, I chose to continue living with gusto—I wouldn't cheat life.

Chapter 2
Keep Moving

April 8th, 1962: My birth

On that momentous date, my mother, Susan, then eight months pregnant, faced three life-or-death struggles.

Her husband, Ernest, had already been hospitalized with late-stage colon cancer when she noticed early labor signs. Susan herself rushed to the nearest emergency room, at Elmhurst Hospital, a municipal facility in Queens. After an examination, the medical staff wanted to check her in for a premature delivery.

My mother refused to be admitted to Elmhurst, where she considered the care substandard. Instead, she took a taxi to Forest Hills General Hospital, her will to survive bolstered by newfound maternal instincts.

The final life-and-death struggle was my own. Born six weeks premature, I started life that day in a neonatal incubator. When I was strong enough, my mother moved me to Mount Sinai Hospital—where my father fought for his life—so she could keep an eye on both of us as she recovered.

Within two months, Ernest succumbed to his cancer, casting a shadow of grief and sorrow over the joys of new motherhood.

Susan Cooper, perennial survivor—the girl who had escaped Auschwitz to forge her own life in New York—had to once again find her way alone. This time with a new soul to nurture to adulthood.

Her troubles didn't end there. Less than eight years later, when I was in third grade, Susan underwent a mastectomy and survived her first brush with breast cancer.

By the end of her life, when she was sixty-eight, my mother had faced more hardships than one person should be allowed to bear. The only (somewhat wry, sarcastic) explanation I could come up with at the time was that God must let the strongest people suffer the most; testing those with the strength and will to endure.

Looking back, I realize my comment had little to do with God or religion and more to do with recognizing my mother's survivor mindset. Despite outrageous loss and seemingly insurmountable hurdles, Susan always pushed on, tackling every obstacle in her path with quiet resolution and strength of mind.

How did she do it?

Now I know the answer: she didn't give herself the option of giving up, standing still, or even slowing down. While she never expressed this sentiment, I know it to be true. I can hear the words reverberating silently in my head even now: "I didn't have a choice."

There will always be forks in the road. Moments to choose between resilience and fragility, courage or despair. "Having no choice" means denying all options except the one that lets you move forward. That is exactly how my mother lived her life, abiding by what I sometimes call the "Cooper Rule."

Never stagnate and never give up. Just *keep moving*—and the path will appear.

As a survivor—or the child of survivors—you learn early on that there's no time to waste in contemplation or rumination. When you can't afford to analyze every possible outcome, you lean into gut instincts and move through challenges with conviction.

This rule keeps me forging ahead despite my terminal diagnosis. When friends ask how I remain positive, upbeat, and active, I tell them I simply have no choice. Like my mother, it's not an option to indulge in self-pity or change how I live.

Surviving is part of my DNA. It's who I am.

Solo Ventures

After my father's funeral, Susan traveled with her newborn infant to Jacksonville, Florida, to visit her brother, Martin, and plan her next move. As the oldest sibling, Martin was the family elder. He suggested we move to Florida for support or even consider temporary foster care for me while my mother got back on her feet. Susan chose neither option. Instead, we flew back to New York City, where she rebuilt our lives from the ashes of death.

First, she had to get back to work. Resourceful as ever, she landed a manicurist job at a beauty parlor called Harold's and proceeded to redefine her life—visually represented by her switch from dark brunette to the blond I would always know her as. Later, she also took clients out of our small, one-bedroom apartment in Forest Hills—where she could keep one eye on me and one on her customers' nails. Until then, she hired a Puerto Rican caretaker named Ortensia, who shared our tiny Queens apartment during the week.

Ortensia didn't speak a word of English. No problem; before long, my mother was adding Spanish to her linguistic repertoire, along with the combination of Hungarian, Yiddish, Hebrew, and Czech she'd needed in the wake of both the Austro-Hungarian Empire and the Second World War. During these early years, I remember saying *cabeza* for "head" and *baño* for "bath."

I spent a lot of time quietly unattended. I'd crawl between chairs and lie under our dining room table—my own secret, enclosed world—lost in my head. Early on, I learned to block out thoughts, even questions, about the father I never knew and the mother who worked so much and talked so little about herself or our family. Instead, I followed threads of imagination where, like her, I could forge ahead, brave and resolute.

After we moved to a nicer, middle-class neighborhood in Forest Hills, Queens, I started kindergarten, followed by first grade in the Jewish parochial school, Yeshiva Dov Revel.

Finally—the chance to interact with other kids and see how I stacked up! Was I going to be a shy or popular kid? Was I someone you'd choose for your team on the playground? Was I smart enough to hold my own?

It took me until junior high—even high school—to fully answer these questions. Let's just say that in elementary school, I hadn't yet perfected that "Cooper Rule" of decisive confidence and grit.

One thing I did know was I was different: the son of a dead father and immigrant mother—both Holocaust survivors. Unlike most other moms, mine worked full-time. She couldn't help with any homework—except Hebrew—and she couldn't even drive.

Plus, at just six-and-a-half years old, I was the youngest in my first-grade class, so the school administration put me on the "C" track with all the kids who struggled to pay attention or keep up. By sixth grade, I'd moved up through "B" and "A" tracks to join the "smart kids," but the damage to my psyche had been done.

A latchkey child, I'd ride the school bus home with our apartment key tied to a shoelace around my neck. Then I'd spend more time alone, doing homework or watching TV until Mom got home.

Outside of the bus route, my minuscule universe extended from the corner of 68th Drive and Queens Boulevard to Yellowstone Boulevard and 68th Road. Because the Yeshiva bused students from all over Queens, I navigated two networks: the kids in these two city blocks and schoolmates—aside from my neighborhood friend, Steve, who was one year ahead of me at Yeshiva.

Aside from Steve, I didn't fit in so easily with my middle-class Jewish classmates. They weren't cruel or even excessively cliquish; I just somehow felt outside of the action, looking in. Since I was used to keeping my own company, that was alright with me.

This self-imposed solitude led me to my first and lifelong musical love, fellow Jerseyite Bruce Springsteen. I used to eat my lunch quickly in the cafeteria, then sneak over to the school library, which I knew would be empty. I also knew it had a record player and the—to me, priceless—record, *Darkness at the Edge of Town*.

I'd carefully pull that black disc out of its paper sleeve, blow off the dust, and gently set the needle down, letting the warm crackle of vinyl and Springsteen's soulful, gritty lyrics wash over me. This album felt darker and more brooding than his previous work, but somehow it connected just right, cementing my love for music. These songs spoke to my soul, helping me realize I could go my own way in the world.

One reason why I didn't quite fit in was that my mother and I were not observant religious Jews. On Saturdays, while most other parents in the Yeshiva went with their children to synagogue for the Jewish Sabbath, my mother headed to the beauty parlor for her busiest day.

After Sabbath morning services alone, I'd promptly jump out of my *shul* (i.e., synagogue) clothes and head straight to the schoolyard playground for some stickball, softball, and basketball. This Saturday routine usually ended with me back in our apartment alone, watching TV.

That is, until the age of about twelve, when I, too, became industrious on the Sabbath. I still went to morning services, but then I'd dash up the block to the corner beauty parlor where my mother worked on Queens Boulevard, take lunch orders from the staff and customers, and run two blocks to fill them at the luncheonette. After returning with my sack full of brown paper bags, I could collect a tidy sum of $10 or more in tips—not a bad haul.

This kid from Queens was learning to hustle, and I liked the fruits of my labor.

Camp Leah

It would take me until college to fully hit my stride and feel confidence and belonging—but there was one time of year when I felt like a different kid: sleepaway camp.

At Camp Leah, I was no quiet, secular immigrant's kid blending in with the scenery. There, I felt like a top dog.

Nestled on idyllic Lake Tiorati in Harriman, New York, Camp Leah was truly a Shangri-La for a city kid like me. Run by the Educational Alliance, a 130-year-old historically Jewish organization on the Lower East Side of Manhattan, it aimed to provide educational, social, and cultural programs to young New Yorkers of all stripes and colors: a classic New York City melting pot of kids from different races, religions, and socioeconomic strata.

Something about Camp Leah—so far removed from my day-to-day reality in Queens—brought out some latent confidence within me. In the two hours it took camp buses to drive from the Lower East Side of Manhattan, through the Lincoln Tunnel, and down old Route 17 into Harriman Park, I transformed from Yeshiva misfit to big man on campus.

For six straight years, I spent summers at Camp Leah, playing sports, socializing with girls, and adopting the swagger of richer, smarter kids. For nine weeks, aside from a few visiting days and weekends between three-week sessions, I didn't see my mother at all. The only communications allowed were postcards, letters—and the occasional collect call I'd sneak from a public payphone on Fridays when our bunk hiked to a full-service public beach.

At the end of each summer when I returned home, I'd get off the camp bus to find my mother waiting with a hug and kiss. After not hearing her voice all summer, my mom's heavily accented, *"Hello, O-lex,"* always startled me for a moment. She sounded *foreign*, even to me. I never felt embarrassed by my mother—in fact, I was proud of her strength and hard work. Still, moments like these reinforced my belief that I was somehow different from my peers.

Over the Outfield Fence

While not rich, I don't recall feeling poor growing up. Through a combination of scholarships, volunteer work, and grit, Mom sent me to an elite private Hebrew high school in Manhattan, and I'd go on to attend one of the top liberal arts colleges in the country.

Because my mother worked so hard, we didn't lack much. We took vacations like other families—weekend trips to the Catskills, Disney parks in Florida and California, and even trips by air to England and Israel. Though I recall clashing with my mother over stylish clothes I wanted, she eventually got me the same suede Pro-Keds sneakers and white painter pants the other kids wore.

I now realize that only self-imposed boundaries kept me from fully thriving in my yeshiva life. Unlike in most Hebrew schools, my yeshivas were both co-ed, so had I not convinced myself that dating religious girls "wasn't cool," I might have socialized more, and even gone on some dates.

Fitting in is a big deal to any kid. I couldn't change my mother's thick Hungarian accent, nor did I want to. But my first taste of "the American dream" was pure and simple.

Though I couldn't at first play—or even fully understand it—I fell head over heels in love with baseball.

Nothing felt more *American*. The fact that my adopted team from Queens were lovable losers and underdogs that everybody adored made sense to me, too. It felt like an omen from the *baseball gods* that I was born in the same year, month, and zip code as our New York Mets.

Baseball was in my blood—I could *feel it*, immigrant's kid or not.

I so badly wanted to go to a Mets game, but with no father to teach me to throw or take me to Shea Stadium, my chances were slim at first. When the "Miracle Mets" won the 1969 World Series, I was oblivious.

Finally, after I turned twelve, my mother let a neighborhood friend take me to my first Mets game. After that, we started catching the subway to Shea or riding our bikes through Flushing Meadows Park to sneak peeks at the ball field from the 7-train subway platform, perched high enough to see over the outfield fence.

I didn't really consider myself an athlete, although I did spend some years playing Sunday games in a Jewish Little League organized by local area synagogues, as well as (non-varsity) softball in high school. Somehow those more formal experiences paled in comparison to those early years in the schoolyards of Forest Hills, spending every last minute of spring and summer daylight playing stickball on school playgrounds with no grass.

By the time my mom would get off work, she had little energy left over for quality time—but I don't remember ever feeling unloved. Nor do I ever remember an encounter with other adults where she couldn't hold her own—despite coming to the United States with only a grade school education, no English, and no familiarity with the norms of this urbane, secular society.

My mother, born in the wrong time and place, proved herself to be a modern, progressive woman. But then, when survival meant always keeping your head high and your stride strong, forward was the only option.

On Faith and Duty

After eighth grade, it was time to complete my Yeshiva education. Like Steve, who had graduated from Yeshiva the year before, I wanted to attend the public Forest Hills High School—but my mother had other ideas.

Even though we were not observant, she wanted me to continue at a Yeshiva High School, believing it would keep me away from typical teenage temptations of booze and drugs. Grudgingly, I admit she was not entirely wrong.

We argued, and I dug in. But eventually, we reached a Solomonic compromise—without requiring us to split the baby. There was one Yeshiva High School I would consider. Ramaz was modern and progressive, on par with the best college prep schools in New York City, but it required an entrance exam. So, I promised Mom I would take the test. If I passed, I'd go to Ramaz. Otherwise, I'd go to public school with Steve.

Not only did I pass the test, but I received a scholarship to boot. I could have purposely bombed the entrance exam, securing my desired spot at the public high school with my best friend. However, the thought never seriously crossed my mind; I could never intentionally disappoint my mother.

Mom and I depended on each other. I needed her unconditional love, physical and emotional sustenance, and a roof over my head. She relied on me to be a good kid to repay her efforts by forging a much better life for myself than she had.

I understood that providing for me, and even living her life through mine, fueled my mother's sense of purpose and redeemed those missed opportunities and connections so cruelly taken from her. It would never have occurred to me to let her down—nor did I want to. I made good on an unspoken vow to do my best for her. As far as I was concerned, there were zero options aside from becoming her dutiful son, working hard in school, and avoiding drugs and trouble.

Besides, I couldn't fail that high school entrance exam. I had to prove I was just as smart as the rich Park Avenue kids who attended Ramaz. But while getting into Ramaz felt like an achievement, I held on to my outsider identity—and the chip on my shoulder and feeling of having something to prove. The comedian Groucho Marx best sums up my attitude at the time: "I refuse to join any club that would have me as a member."

I made very few friends at Ramaz, in part because of the transportation logistics of meeting up for parties, games, or other events without a car. But I did get a quality secular and Jewish education, including mastering Hebrew and developing a love for studying the Torah (Old Testament Bible) and the Talmud, a collection of Jewish stories, teachings, and laws. Still, my experiences and beliefs differed from those of my classmates; I remained, like my mother, essentially secular. My faith remained rooted in my duty to honor my mother's sacrifices and efforts.

New Horizons

As a teenager, inconsequential choices can feel daunting and huge. Should I ask this girl for a date? Which friend should I call tonight? Am I ready to try out for the varsity team?

Looking back, my first decision of real consequence was selecting a college.

The world of college life was as foreign to my mother as the first time she saw the Statue of Liberty in the New York harbor, so I mostly figured out college admissions alone.

Steve was already attending Columbia University, but when they rejected me for early admission, he suggested Vassar College in Poughkeepsie, New York. My mother preferred Brandeis University, on the outskirts of Boston, given what she'd heard about its strong Jewish heritage and strong computer science program. Still, I was hell-bent on Vassar. Originally founded in 1861 as a women's college, Vassar ranked among the most liberal and progressive schools in the country.

When Mom's neighborhood friend (who had kids at Vassar) offered to drive me to Poughkeepsie for a visit and college tour, my mother agreed to let me go—but she didn't come along.

The instant I stepped foot on Vassar's bucolic campus, I was smitten. All those tree-lined, emerald-green lawns and Collegiate Gothic old buildings just oozed "liberal arts education" to me. The cute, sassy female tour guide who showed me around campus clinched the deal.

Vassar was it for me. Once again, there were no other options, no "fallback" or reason to consider a plan B.

It was time to leave my small-minded, secluded, semi-religious world behind and expand my horizons. This time, there would be no Solomonic compromise. My mother relied on sources telling her that Brandeis was the "safer choice." I relied on pure instinct. We could not agree, so I respectfully told her it was my decision. I would be going to Vassar.

Yogi Berra, one of the all-time greatest New York Yankees baseball players, said it best; "When you come to a fork in the road, take it!" My translation of Yogi's quirky but sage advice is this:

If you follow your gut to choose a direction, it will be the right one.

In the last week of August 1979, I packed up an old army duffle bag full of clothing and took a train from Grand Central Station in Manhattan to Poughkeepsie. A week later, my mother hitched a ride from a friend to bring the rest of my things and help me settle into my new life.

Gut Instincts

Having fully grown into the "Cooper Rule," I followed my gut when I picked my college path—and I've followed it through every important decision I've made since. I knew I had the confidence and will to follow my convictions because I'd learned from my mother's quick, decisive ways. From insisting on my birth at Forest Hills General Hospital to hiring Ortensia and sending me to Yeshiva schools, she always leaned into her instincts and maintained forward momentum.

Like her, I grew to be willful, resourceful, and resilient. Luckily, I didn't have to lose my parents and grandparents, become homeless, switch countries (multiple times), and navigate daily life-and-death situations to develop these character traits. I remain forever grateful for my mother's devotion, her sacrifices, and all her hard work.

Necessity is the mother of invention, but dire situations don't guarantee confidence or strength of character. Susan Cooper walked the world alone, and—in a much quieter, gentler way—my childhood felt much the same. But instead of becoming lonely, I learned to rely on myself.

This innate confidence and decisiveness would go on to carry me to great heights. Part of it came down to my inherited, compulsive need for constant forward motion—a trait common to both Holocaust survivors and their children. Whether hiding in a crawl space, enduring forced death marches in Eastern Europe, or stepping off the train in

Auschwitz, survivors like my mother had to keep moving—physically or mentally—to feel safe. I developed this feeling too. Without exaggeration, remaining still or stagnant felt to me like a risk of death.

I would follow this instinct throughout college and into my career, helping me navigate everything from corporate life to family life to Ironman races—that is, until I got cancer. Quite honestly, waiting to schedule that damn MRI represents one of the few moments of serious hesitation in my entire life.

Following the chilling confirmation of a brain tumor, I did move quickly toward treatment—but I took my time in one respect: sharing the news. I'd always preferred *solving* problems to *sharing* them, at least until I'd already devised and implemented solutions to said problems. That wasn't going to be an option in this situation, and I needed to process and accept that fact.

Meanwhile, Beth and the kids still saw me as the strong, unwavering head of the household—always in motion and fully in command of his destiny. Ironclad, steadfast, even indestructible.

Once they knew the results of the test, that story would change.

Chapter 3
Own the Narrative

January 6, 2023: The MRI

The MRI taken on this date confirmed the news. I guess it's hard to miss a mass the size of a clementine. This was certainly not the new challenge I'd had in mind that day while swimming Madison's Lake Monona, pondering my future—but it's the one I got.

There's no getting around it. It's a gut punch finding out you have a tumor growing in your skull. But there's also no better wake-up call. It was time to take stock and gather intel.

Was the growth malignant, and if so, what type of cancer was it? Had it spread to other parts of my body? Would it? What would be my next step?

While I'd have to wait a bit for answers and proper treatments, I had no time to waste in living a meaningful life—every single moment. Especially with this new specter of death hanging around, I was determined to make every day count. There's a quote I always liked, apocryphally attributed to Abraham Lincoln: "In the end, it's not the years in your life that count, but the life in your years."

I'd long harbored the deep, dark secret belief that, like my parents, I would someday face a cancer diagnosis. I kept that premonition buried and protected my whole life. Now I no longer had the luxury of hiding my fate or fears in the shadows—or anyway, not for long.

After the second MRI, I called my internal medicine physician to share the results and discuss next steps. There was a small possibility the tumor was benign, but given my family history, I wasn't getting my hopes up. The recommended course of action was definitive and clear: I needed to see a neurosurgeon immediately.

So, what did I do next?

Two days after the second MRI, I hopped on a plane to Belize with Beth. And, at least for the duration of that trip—I made the decision to keep the results to myself.

She and I had planned this vacation months earlier. We'd been to Belize once before and vowed to return after COVID-19 restrictions relaxed. Belize was our happy place, our beautiful Caribbean paradise. Now, more than ever, I needed that trip—a peaceful, sunny oasis with my wife.

Until this point, I'd kept Beth abreast of every symptom, doctor's appointment, and potential for good or bad news. I wanted to include my loving partner and life companion in this journey. After all, she needed to know how much my life and hers were about to change.

I also knew she'd do the smart, sensible thing and postpone our vacation—even though going would not delay my medical care. Sure, my neurologist had put me on an anti-seizure drug, but he called it "a precaution," so I chose not to worry. Getting referrals, finding a surgeon, and scheduling the initial consultation with the neurosurgeon would take at least a week or two. I could manage that process from Belize.

Even if Beth had agreed to the trip, knowing my medical status, the news would have cast a cloud so dark and thick that no rum punch on the beach would lift the shadows.

Besides, once news gets out, everything changes fast. I needed time to anchor myself into this new reality—to ground into the internal strength and support that I and everyone around me needed.

This leads me to the second principle of my IronCEO mindset: *Own the narrative.*

Life throws a lot of curveballs, but your reaction—the story you tell yourself—is always up to you. With enough conviction, you can maintain a sense of authorship, even when the plotline takes a dreadful twist beyond your control.

My self-imposed news embargo offered a much-needed benefit. I knew I'd lose this calm command of the storyline upon sharing the news with loved ones. Doctors, hospitals, surgeries, treatment regimens, prognoses, and outcomes would become my new life.

Above all, I worried about the impact on my wife and grown children. I wanted time to process my emotions and prepare for this next chapter in my life—before I could bring them along. When the time was right, I wanted them to hear the story of their trusted father and husband, a man who'd prepared his whole life for this challenge. A man who was ready.

Until then, I held my tongue—and took my wife on the trip of a lifetime.

Belize or Bust

After flying into Belize City airport, we took a small pedal jumper plane to the beach where we'd stay. Something about sitting shotgun on that tiny, vintage-looking aircraft shifted my perspective. It felt like we'd stepped through a portal to a temporary, alternative reality where I could breathe more easily. Once again, I vowed to make the most of these final days before everything changed.

For the most part, I succeeded in protecting the beautiful Caribbean cabanas, beachside drinks, and moments of contemplative calm from my new—and fast-encroaching—reality. I did have to sneak emails and phone calls to medical providers in Denver, who scrambled to get referrals and appointments with neurosurgeons. And, of course, I had to evade Beth's intermittent questioning about the results of my MRI.

While never fully out of mind, I managed to compartmentalize my feelings and fears as we relished low-key dinners of rock lobsters, fried plantain, and cod tacos, often purchased at roadside stands after driving a golf cart forty-five minutes past the resort traps to explore local dives. One evening our carefree roving even got us stranded in dark, unlit streets, forcing us to abandon the golf cart overnight and hail a taxi home, laughing as we went.

During the day, we'd lounge by the sea or rent a boat to paddle out among the turquoise-blue Caribbean waves. Beth, who didn't enjoy deep swims, would stay in the boat while I dove in to snorkel among the world's second-largest barrier reef.

Drifting gently among tropical fish, colorful corals, and undulating sea grass, I savored those moments of serenity and gratitude, at peace with my life and ready to make the most of every second that remained.

Despite my success in hiding the big secret, I was not a good liar. While I managed to conceal my swirling emotions, Beth grew increasingly suspicious as the vacation drew to a close. The headline of my illness, currently written with invisible ink, weighed heavily on me.

Back to Reality

As soon as we boarded our flight home from Belize, I began thinking about how to tell Beth and the kids about the tumor. There's never a good time or place to tell the ones you love such upsetting news.

As soon as we got home and deposited our luggage from the trip, I sat Beth down in the living room. Luckily, she wasn't mad that I'd kept this life-changing information to myself. But that didn't mean the moment went without a deep sense of dread. I remember the flash of disbelief and helplessness in her eyes, just before the tears began falling and I gathered her into my arms.

The next day, my two grown children, Jess and Evan—both Colorado transplants, like Beth and me—came over for dinner and were served the same appetite-suppressing update, followed by more tears and hugs, sadness and shock. We had to break the bad news over the phone to my stepchildren, Ben and Molly, who lived on the East Coast.

Unfortunately, I had ample experience in delivering bad news. I told my kids when they were six and eight years old about their grandmother's passing. I also delivered the devastating news that the girlfriend I'd been seeing for years after my divorce had died in an accident while biking with me. There's no way to sugarcoat heartache. All you can do is let the words flow from your lips succinctly and compassionately, offer an embrace, and hold space for tears to flow.

Bedside Manner

With my family in the loop, it was time to forge ahead with treatment solutions. My friends in the medical community had warned me that surgeons often lack bedside manner, but that first consultation with a neurosurgeon caught me off guard anyway. He failed to introduce himself to Beth or look either of us in the eyes, and he delivered the news about my prognosis and life expectancy in a tone of chilling, matter-of-fact indifference.

I get that surgeons detach emotionally to execute their jobs with elite technical precision—and, of course, I wanted the most skilled, specialized surgeon to fix my high-performance brain—but not at the cost of basic human connection and trust. Normally so grounded and composed, I felt myself break into a cold sweat as this surgeon spoke. When we left the office, Beth mentioned that I looked pale. I could barely conceal the shaking in my hands. Needless to say, we crossed that surgeon off the list.

No problem. From the outset of this selection process, "Plan A" was to get an appointment at the main teaching hospital for the University of Colorado (CU) School of Medicine.

After ten days of waiting and pulling every string we could find, we finally booked a consultation with the CU Medical Center neurology team on January 19—after a CU committee assessed my case to determine the likelihood of at least extending my life.

Beth and I felt immediately comfortable with the medical team, hospital, and process at CU. First, the resident physician introduced himself to Beth and me, making sure he looked us both in the eyes and learned our full names before asking questions—not just about my medical history, but about our family, work, and personal passions.

My decades of high-stakes sales calls, networking, and investor presentations paled in comparison to the importance of this interview and selection process. Still, my background did help me prepare for the moment. During my career, I always put my customers and their company interests first. I wouldn't have won a single deal if my customers didn't trust me—no matter how good the product or how great a company was. I now applied that same criteria to picking out the right surgical team.

Before putting my life in someone's hands, I needed *trust*—based not only on a dispassionate, objective analysis of qualifications, but also on a felt sense of honesty, integrity, and mutual interest.

Since trust is a two-way street, I also wanted the doctors to understand who they were dealing with—a patient with the physical stamina, mental fortitude, confidence, and resilience to overcome challenges—one who habitually challenged himself, as well as placed restrictions on his health and exercise regimen.

After fifteen minutes, the resident left and returned with the neurosurgeon assigned to my case. As expected, the surgeon walked in with a warm *hello* and confident swagger. He introduced himself to us both and shook our hands before asking friendly questions about our lives—with the same personal, human approach. Only then did he present the medical facts, showing MRI images of the ugly mass and describing the craniotomy procedure on the left frontal lobe of my brain with clarity and sensitivity.

We had found my medical team.

Eyes Wide Open

One aspect of owning the narrative involves compartmentalizing feelings and information to avoid mental overwhelm. Although curious and well-educated, I wanted to manage the amount and type of information I received about my cancer. On one hand, I took a keen interest in discussing the surgical process and risk factors. I wanted to fully understand the mechanics of opening my skull, including what could go wrong.

The last thing I wanted to hear were facts and figures about success rates and life expectancies.

Thinking about myself and my life as statistics didn't empower me. For endurance races like triathlons, I only ever competed against myself—no other numbers had ever concerned me. Since my story was the only one that mattered in this situation, the only patient outcomes I cared about were my own.

Rather than sterile data and probabilities, I needed to focus on what was possible. I could not control all the variables and outcomes involved, but I could at least control my beliefs and attitudes. Positivity goes a long way—and it certainly beats anxiety and fear.

Speaking of things I could control; I had a decision to make. I could either remain awake for most of my four-to five-hour procedure or get sedated with general anesthesia for the duration. I was intrigued by the prospect of observing and assisting the process—especially after the doctors explained how I could help.

While an MRI provides a clear map of a tumor's location and size, it doesn't tell the surgeon whether the surrounding brain tissue is safe to remove. Since the first principle of the Hippocratic oath is "do no harm," surgeons avoid impacting important brain functions as much as possible. My tumor was growing on my left parietal lobe, an area involved in speech, processing sensory information, and navigating through space.

Although I wouldn't feel anything because the brain lacks pain receptors, the scalp would be anesthetized so the surgeon could test my speech and other cognitive functions by stimulating parts of my brain tissue and asking me questions as they worked. This would help the team understand which brain tissue might seriously impact my cognitive abilities.

Being awake and aware while doctors poke around in your brain may sound terrifying, but it gave me great comfort to know that I could influence the outcome of my surgery. I knew my IronCEO mindset would make it possible for me to stay calm and alert for three hours in the operating theater, surrounded by surgeons, anesthesiologists, nurses, and a speech therapist.

Besides, the post-op recovery would be easier and faster without general anesthesia. For me, the decision to stay awake was (excusing my pun) a classic no-brainer.

Ironman Face

The last stop before surgery involved yet another visit to the confining cylinder of the MRI machine, this time to create a baseline map of critical speech and cognitive functions. Inside the machine, I listened to prompts and stared at a tablet-sized computer screen flashing images of words—some were logical sentences I had to complete and others were pure nonsense. This measured my brain activity when actively thinking and at rest.

While lying in that noisy metallic tube, I felt myself instinctively put on my "Ironman face." According to my wife and kids, my signature game face expression always emerged in the final minutes before I dove into open water to begin an Ironman race. It reflected the IronCEO mindset grounded in completing each swim stroke, pedal revolution, or running stride.

To truly own the narrative, you can't let the enormity of a situation overwhelm you. You have to anchor into the present moment and your own confidence. Rather than putting all your faith in externals, it's crucial to fully show up and direct your own course—and that means trusting yourself to meet each moment.

I've certainly been guilty of overdoing it, using work and exercise as an emotional salve. But even if I raced daily triathlons, exertion and busyness alone wouldn't keep me in the moment. The mind is porous, allowing doubts and negative thoughts to creep in. Besides, no one can swim, bike, and run dozens of miles every day. To battle cancer, I'd face unprecedented physical restrictions.

I needed to learn one final, foolproof technique.

The final key to owning the narrative involves understanding what you can and cannot control. There will always be unforeseen variables and obstacles to alternately address, accept, and adapt to. You have to learn the art of committing to goals without attachment to outcomes. When I started racing triathlons, I certainly had both goals and expectations. I wanted to constantly improve and advance, race to race and year to year.

These days, I no longer even think of triathlon as a "race" in the traditional sense because where I place and when I finish—neither matters anymore. Only two things motivate me: my commitment to preparing for the race and putting my feet in the water to start the initial swim.

Athletes commonly experience tunnel vision as a mental tool for staying in the moment. We call it "being in the zone." During high-stress events, I've learned to tune out non-essential information, and the days leading up to surgery were no exception.

I had to get in the zone to prepare myself for all I would experience on the day of the surgery, both physically and emotionally. But without the benefit of competitors in triathlon suits and cheering crowds—without even work deadlines to occupy my thoughts—this could get tricky.

That's how I knew I made the right decision in going to Belize. That trip provided the luxury of time and space for me to gather my thoughts and process the situation. Looking back on those peaceful moments snorkeling through coral reefs, adventurous Caribbean golf cart rides, and carefree beach strolls, I knew I'd given myself and Beth a priceless gift.

I remain forever grateful for that week of bliss, beauty, and love in Belize before the whirlwind of hope, agony, resilience, and despair became our new reality.

When I returned to Denver and shared the diagnosis with close friends, some were incredulous that I kept this closely guarded secret from Beth during our trip (and my neurologist friend, understanding the risks of my conditions and ramifications of dealing with health issues outside of the country, was furious).

But I never doubted I could compartmentalize emotions and enjoy a much-needed vacation with my beautiful wife. My life experiences taught me to block out noise—to think clearly and act decisively. I'm sure I would not have been able to start even one company, much less three businesses, if I'd listened to all the critics and naysayers.

In my decades of both business and endurance racing, I've learned to focus on the journey, not the finish line. To put one foot in front of the other. By reducing the undue pressure of expectations, the path became energizing and even joyful—despite pain, fatigue, and setbacks along the way.

In the days leading up to my surgery, it was time to put on my "Ironman face" and apply this same mindset to cancer. I knew I could pull it off. Not only because of the life I'd led, but because of the endurance and fortitude in my very DNA, inherited from an ancestral line of fierce survivors.

Chapter 4
I Am a Survivor

January 27, 1945: The liberation of Auschwitz

Soviet troops advanced into Auschwitz, Poland, on this date, liberating more than 6,000 remaining Jewish prisoners from the Nazi's largest concentration and death camp—among them, my seventeen-year-old mother and her fifteen-year-old sister, Chaya.

This and other seminal events that would go on to shape my outlook on life occurred long before I was conceived. As the son of Holocaust survivors, learning about the past was more than a history lesson. It was an opportunity to look in the mirror and see who I am.

As a young boy, I knew nothing of my mother's story or the fate of her parents, grandparents, and other family members, all of whom perished in the Holocaust.

Despite having bona fide survivors for parents, I barely knew what the Holocaust was until the fourth grade when I attended my first school assembly for *Yom Ha Ziharon*, the Day of Remembrance. Until that day, the word "Holocaust" had been a dark, abstract notion—one never brought up at home, except perhaps in Hungarian or Czech whispers between my mother and fellow survivors.

It's easy now to regret not asking my mother more questions about her life. But as a child, I sensed deep pain in the silence surrounding her past experiences and instinctively avoided such topics. This included the topic of my father—that man in the faded photograph, holding me, his newborn baby, mere months before he succumbed to cancer. It unnerved me how skinny and sickly my father looked in that photo, as though he'd never left the Mauthausen concentration camp in Austria where he'd been sent away from his Hungarian homeland in his early twenties.

Although much of my family heritage remains a black box, the tragedy of six million Jews perishing at the hands of Nazis and other willing collaborators reverberates from generation to generation. The impact will be felt for eternity.

The Holocaust didn't just make my parents survivors; it made me a survivor, too. It's in my DNA, passing through generational struggles and tenacity to reach me.

I was a survivor long before I got cancer.

I was a survivor before my girlfriend of several years was killed in a bike accident right before my eyes.

I was a survivor before my first wife and I split after ten years of marriage, before I packed my duffel bag and boarded a train to Poughkeepsie for Vassar College, and even before my earliest boyhood days daydreaming alone beneath our dining room table.

That survivor gene has kept me going through my life-and-death struggle with cancer. While I didn't face the hardships and dangers my parents endured, their instincts and will to survive lived on through me and my children.

My mother and her siblings came out of the war irrevocably changed. Bearing scars and concentration camp numbers tattooed on their arms—plus much deeper, invisible wounds. Many survivors struggled to adapt, unable to sleep without nightmares, maintain social relationships, or function in society.

Others, like my mother and her siblings, proved better at hiding their secrets and scars. To me, they seemed well-adjusted and resilient, embodying what psychologists call "post-traumatic growth" by blooming in the harshest of soils.

For Holocaust survivors, there's no greater act of defiance than finding a spouse, creating a family, and raising the next generation of Jewish children to thrive. This goal required all my mother's energy and focus as I grew up. The silver lining was that these efforts did not leave much time to wallow in the past or worry about the future.

Even as a young boy, I inherited threads of their well-earned grit as well as a sense of duty and responsibility to my single mother—to always do the right thing and stay out of trouble.

This included not asking too many questions.

However, part of my own survivorship involved applying courage to curiosity and defiantly excavating what little I could out of the rubble of the past. Through a journey of research and discovery, I managed to uncover that mirror into my family's past—for better or worse—to honor my estranged family history and my birthright as a survivor.

Finding the Lost

In 2006, while accompanying my son, Evan, on a college visit in Providence, Rhode Island, I wandered into a bookstore and stumbled upon a serendipitous gem: *The Lost: A Search for Six of Six Million* by Daniel Mendelsohn. The book described the writer's struggle to piece together the tragic account of his relatives who perished in the Holocaust—inspiring me to do the same.

Like the author, I was haunted by gaping holes in my family history. Very little information remained about the author's family—much like mine: the Coopers (originally *Kupfersteins*), Tabaks (my mother's maiden name), and Shlomovitzs (my maternal grandmother's maiden name), to name a few.

When these relatives lost their lives, the world lost their hopes, aspirations, stories, futures, and unborn branches of their family trees. With some sleuthing, including visits to the US Holocaust Museum, talks with my uncles, and correspondence with an amateur genealogist and distant relative, I managed to at least round up some basic facts.

Susan Cooper—then Susan Tabak—entered the Auschwitz-Birkenau concentration camp in May 1944. Before that, she and Aunt Chaya had been separated from her parents and five brothers and forced into a ghetto—along with some 18,000 other Jews—in Mateszalka, a town about ninety miles west of her birthplace of Solotvina.

Though originally a Hungarian *shtetl* or Jewish settlement, Solotvina became a part of Czechoslovakia in 1920, only to be returned to Hungary in 1939 and then annexed by the Soviet Union as part of Ukraine following World War II.

Within these shifting borders, Susan and her family had learned adaptability and grit—not to mention Hungarian and Czech, in addition to the Yiddish and Hebrew they'd spoken and read at home.

The day Auschwitz was liberated—revealing the full horrors of the Nazi's murderous regime to the world—my father, Ernest Kupferstein (anglicized by immigration officers to "Cooper"), was still in the Mauthausen concentration camp in Austria. He was finally freed in April 1945.

"Erno" Cooper, as he was called, also hailed from a Hungarian town—though he and Susan wouldn't meet until more than a decade later after both of them moved to the Forest Hills neighborhood of Queens, New York.

The Aftermath

Even before the war, my ancestors faced generations of poverty, suffering, and persecution by Germans, Russians, Ukrainians, Cossacks, and more. Still, living in Hungary was the closest thing to a lottery ticket for Eastern European Jews during World War II. As the last major population of Jews deported to concentration camps, Hungarian Jews managed to survive in greater numbers.

After SS troops initially separated my family, they were dispersed among various displaced persons (DP) camps. My uncles were sent to work camps, struggling to survive the brutal cold, lack of food, hard labor, and the constant threat of being shot by a soldier for the crime of being a Jew—before ending up in concentration camps themselves.

In the immediate aftermath of the Allies' victory, my mother and her siblings scoured the lists of survivors provided by American and Jewish agencies posted in towns, cities, and the DP camps. They looked in vain for parents, grandparents, and other family members. Only their siblings survived.

At age seventeen, separated from her home, village, and family, these horrific circumstances forced my mother into adulthood with nothing more than a grade school education, the clothes on her back, and her wits.

Before long, she and each of her siblings embarked on intersecting but separate journeys. Uncle Martin immigrated to the United States in 1952. Uncle Jack soon followed, settling in Cleveland, Ohio. My mother, Aunt Chaya, and two remaining uncles, Mike and Iitzik, immigrated to the new state of Israel in 1948, after spending more than a year in various DP camps on mainland Europe—followed by another two in detention camps in Cypress, as the new Jewish state of Israel was being formed.

Anyone who manages to persist through a life-changing ordeal can earn the label "Survivor." However, truly *surviving* the crucible of war or personal tragedy takes more than simply getting through the thing alive. Survival is the beginning—not the endpoint—of the journey.

After losing loved ones and years of her life to anguish—after an experience that broke her heart, spirit, and body—somehow, my mother and her siblings had to pick up the pieces and begin whole new lives, learning new skills, street smarts, and languages; and adapting to foreign environments and cultures.

My mother did this more than once, leaving Israel after about a decade to resettle in New York City. Her sister, Chaya, remained in Israel for the rest of her life.

Upon arriving in the US in 1958, Susan was greeted by her cousin Irving Sloan—also part of the Slomowitz family tree—and his wife, Esther. Though born in the United States, Esther's fluency in Yiddish became my mother's early lifeline to connection and communication. But that would soon change; my polyglot mother picked up English like other people pick up dry cleaning.

After visiting her brothers in Cleveland, Ohio, Susan decided to put down roots in New York City. She settled into the working-class neighborhood of Elmhurst, Queens, found manicurist work at Harold's, and eventually met Ernest, a fellow Hungarian holocaust survivor, who worked as a server in the Mt. Zion Hospital cafeteria. They married in 1960. Unfortunately, I don't know if my mother's brothers or cousins were attending.

As the 1960s began, I'm sure the newlyweds hoped and prayed they could leave their troubles behind and move towards a better future. Despite the blessings of their new life and love, their time together proved sadly short. Within four years, my father died of cancer, mere months after I was born. In 1962, Susan Cooper entered motherhood with one more loss to grieve and survive.

Personal Pilgrimage

My mother's brother, Uncle Jack, lived in the United States for twenty-five years. When he retired, he moved first to Budapest, Hungary, and then to Baia Mare, a city in Northern Romania, barely forty miles from the Southern border with Ukraine in the Carpathian Mountains region near where my mother and her siblings were born.

During a visit to the United States, Jack invited me to Romania and promised to take me to his birthplace. So, five years after my mother died, in March 2002, I took him up on the offer, organizing a trip with two first cousins to visit our ancestral home.

We traveled first to Prague and Budapest by plane. Then after a day-long car trip to Poland to visit the Nazi concentration camps, Buchenwald and Auschwitz-Birkenau, we traveled by train from Budapest through Romania, to Baia Mare. I still recall the austerity of these former Soviet bloc countries. I saw lots of empty shelves and cold, dark rooms, as resources were scarce, including electricity.

We arrived at the train station in Baia Mare to see Uncle Jack in a fedora and long overcoat, cutting a distinctly Humphrey Bogart-like figure through the fog and smell of diesel fuel. I felt like I'd walked right into the final scene of *Casablanca*.

After a few days, Uncle Jack promised to take us to Solotvina, his birthplace, and my mother's—just a short 10-minute drive across the border. He handled the logistics, including hiring a driver with a van to take us through the Carpathian Mountains to the border.

But then, the day before our excursion, Uncle Jack surprised us by announcing he would not come with us the whole way—indeed, he had vowed to never again set foot in Ukraine. Instead, he agreed to drive us to the Sighet, then wait at the border for my cousins and me to take our journey and return. He gave no reason for his refusal to return to Solotvina.

Without Uncle Jack, we'd be traveling blind on our pilgrimage through this small, forgotten Ukrainian village. After getting my hopes up that he'd show us ancestral landmarks and teach us about our family's life in Solotvina, I was crushed. But I knew better than to push Jack for answers or urge him to confront memories of a life he wanted to forget.

As we arrived at the border, the green, sloping Carpathian foothills and the provincial sights and sounds of carts and wagons along misty dirt roads reminded me of the village of Anatevka in *Fiddler on the Roof*.

Finally—I'd made it to my mother's birthplace. Though disappointed to lose my family tour guide, I couldn't wait to finally journey through our ancestral lands.

Sadly, it wasn't meant to be.

Despite having the requested visas and documents to enter Ukraine, when my cousins and I reached Sighet, Romanian border crossing officials refused to admit us. My hustler and wheeler-dealer of an uncle did his best to negotiate and bribe our way across the border in fluent Romanian.

Nothing worked.

There we were, stalled out at a remote border crossing in a former Eastern Bloc communist country. Beyond the requisite visa documents, they kept throwing more red tape. Getting permission from all the appropriate officials and local authorities would take several days at least—and even then, there was no guarantee. My cousins and I reluctantly released our dream of visiting our parents' birthplace.

The main purpose of our mission was now lost, and I felt an unexpected mixture of sadness and relief. Perhaps, I figured, some things were better left unknown. This conclusion fit neatly into the narrative of my family history, where unknowns far outweighed the known.

In 2016, two other cousins ended up successfully visiting Solotvina. There, they found no Jews, no synagogues, and only a few remaining elders with any living memories about the men, women, and children who'd made a home of this long-gone shtetl. No one seemed to remember our family.

Shower of Stars

If something blocks my way, my reaction tends to be fierce and visceral. Whether in business, triathlons, or personal endeavors, I feel my pulse quicken—ready to challenge and overcome obstacles. The speed and single-minded ferocity of this response energizes me. These days, it helps me push forward through my battle with cancer.

The disappointing setback of our family pilgrimage only fueled me to dive head-first into research, scouring family documents to learn more about my heritage. In doing so, I discovered two notable family members.

Elie Wiesel (born Eliezer Wiesel in Sighetu Marmației, Romania, 1928–2016), was an American author, professor, political activist, Nobel laureate, and Holocaust survivor—who penned the famous, hauntingly poetic memoir, *Night*, about his experience as a prisoner in Buchenwald and Auschwitz. Turns out, he was also the second cousin of my mother and her siblings.

The other notable figure, Ian Robert Maxwell MC (born Ján Ludvík Hoch in Solotvina; 1923–1991) was a British and American publishing tycoon who assembled a multi-billion-dollar media empire. Not yet aware of the nazi advancement, Cousin Ian Robert Maxwell and my Uncle Mike escaped

Solotvina and walked through Budapest to find their fame and fortune.

In the biography, *Maxwell*, author Joe Haines, painted a harsh, stirring portrait of Maxwell's early life—and the lives of many of my ancestors. He described Solotvina as a place of "poverty, penury, privation, an endemic, chronic misery from which there was no escape," noting that Maxwell's "abiding, haunting memory of those days is that he was perpetually hungry."

He quotes the well-traveled Maxwell saying, "I have not come across any greater poverty anywhere in the world," before describing a recurring childhood dream of one of his cousins—a dream "of filling his stomach with food and not having to get up in the morning. It seemed to be an impossible dream; daytime's reality was not far from starvation."

Maxwell's wife, Elisabeth Maxwell, Ph.D. (née Meynard, 1921-2013), was a French-born descendant of the Huguenot aristocracy whose distant lineage included kings of France. Dr. Maxwell, herself a survivor, developed a passionate scholarly and personal interest in genealogy and Holocaust remembrance.

What began as a project to prepare a family genealogy for her children evolved into meticulous research, leading her to publish the scholarly journal, *Holocaust and Genocide Studies* and become a leading figure in the field. To do so, she frequently visited with surviving relations, including my mother and her siblings. Most of what I've learned about my family and report here can be attributed to her work.

According to an undated letter she sent my mother, the Maxwell family tree and ours share some common roots. Chaim Leib Slomowitz (born 1818), marks the first record of the Slomowitz name, a bloodline leading to Robert Maxwell's Aunt Sarah—Susan's mother and my maternal grandmother.

Dr. Maxwell compiled all the facts, descriptions, and documents she could from visits to Solotvina when it was still behind the Iron Curtain of the Soviet Union. The resulting compilation featured 1142 entries in her family tree.

In the letter to my mother, Dr. Maxwell wrote: "Of 322 members of your close family who lived in the village at the time of the Holocaust, 169 are known to have perished in the gas chamber, although this number is likely to rise when you have to add your information to mine. Of the 153 who are presumed to have been alive at the liberation, we know of 1/3 who joined the resistance and 1/3 who were deported to Auschwitz or other camps."

When Dr. Maxwell died in 2013, her *New York Times* obituary added a poignant and personal touch to the cold statistics and lists of her genealogy work.

While compiling her family tree, she told *The Guardian* in 2000 that she drew a little star of David "in front of all the people who had been murdered in the camps...And when I unfolded it, it was like a shower of yellow stars."

"I couldn't believe that so many people in one family could have been murdered," she continued. "I just wanted to know why."

Whispers of my Father

Far from fixed objects anchored to the past, memories fluctuate and change. Sometimes due to lost information, sometimes to suit a purpose. The older the memories, the more susceptible it is to distortion or even outright loss. The past eludes in hints, shadows, and whispers.

I'm still haunted by the questions I never asked about my father or my mother's life during the Holocaust. Maybe a sense of duty and compassion toward my mother could justify my reluctance to ask about her own experiences—but why wouldn't I want to know everything I could about my father? I realize now I was hiding behind the idea of protecting my mother's emotions. I avoided the subject for my own sake.

I have very few artifacts from my father, the most notable being a *Mahzor*, a special prayer book containing the liturgy for the High Holidays of Yom Kippur and Rosh Hashana. It was so worn we had to have the cover rebound. The best part is the handwritten inscription on the first page, from my father to my mother. It's an heirloom I cherish. Still, for a long time, I didn't actively seek more information about Ernest Cooper.

I have a complicated relationship with my family's past. While deeply dedicated to closing the knowledge gap about our family origins, there are questions I prefer to keep buried. It's a tightrope of painful secrets and emotional release I've learned to navigate.

'It's hard for me to miss someone I never knew," I used to say when friends asked about my father. Compared to the loss of my mother—or to friends who lost their fathers at a later age—I didn't feel traumatized by growing up without a father: "It's just how my life was."

Those statements were not lies, but I could only make them if I continued to hide behind my lack of information—all those questions never to be asked or answered.

Sometimes, I prefer to block out painful memories, as my mother and her siblings did. They actively avoided talking, or even thinking about, the Holocaust, preferring to forget. My cousin told me how her father—my Uncle Martin—suffered for decades from nightmares and flashbacks. Martin tried so hard to forget his past that he lost the ability to speak his former Hungarian and Yiddish mother tongues.

After receiving my cancer diagnosis, I decided to do all I could to shine light on my father's life and his family. I recently revisited the United States Holocaust Memorial Museum for the first time in probably a decade. During previous visits, I'd made half-hearted attempts to find information on my father—but always gave up quickly, convincing myself there was nothing to find or that it would prove too cumbersome to dig up.

This time, I tapped the support of the museum's amazing research team, including a woman who sat me down and—within ten minutes—found my father's name in their databases.

Ernest Kupferstein (Cooper) was born on July 1, 1922, in Nagykérimajor, Bacs-Kiskun, Hungary, the son of Sarolta and Lajos. His citizenship on immigration papers to the United States is listed as Yugoslavian since the area had been annexed to the new state of Yugoslavia after the First World War. From April 1944 to April 1945, he endured the Mauthausen concentration camp in Austria. After World War II ended, on March 11, 1949, he sailed from Bremerhaven, Germany, to New York on the USS General Muir. In various immigration documents, his occupation was listed as confectioner and driver.

Seeing my father's name and information amid the records of survivors at the Memorial Museum hit me with a mixture of deep gratitude and a tinge of regret for all the missed opportunities to learn more.

More recently, my good friend Sam got in touch with some amateur historians and—in another striking synchronicity—discovered that his uncle, Henry Boehm, had immigrated to New York aboard the very same ship as my dad. Something moved in me when I looked at the photos they sent me of the USS General Muir. Those images connected me to a broader feeling of kinship: to my father, to his fellow survivors and shipmates, and to the families and communities that still grow out of their determination to survive and start over.

To Choose One's Own Way

While shielded from direct experience—and even from stories—about the Holocaust, we children of survivors grew up to become survivors ourselves. When parents struggle through fear, anxiety, or survivor's guilt, children adopt similar ways to overcome, becoming more driven—even defiant—in the face of obstacles.

Like my mother, I proudly and defiantly adopted the term "survivor." This mentality pushed me to do more than merely survive. It drove me to meet any challenge: excelling in school, succeeding in business, raising a family, and even racing in multiple Ironman competitions. I know I'd be strong and resilient without this survivor mentality, but perhaps without the same urgency or clarity of purpose.

Still, it's only in recent years that I've come to appreciate the resilience and sheer force of will required to survive Nazi concentration and death camps. Could you find enough food to keep from starving? Was your body strong enough to withstand hard labor or death marches? Were you resourceful and cunning enough to hide in the forest or the homes of non-Jewish sympathizers?

Answers to these questions helped determine survival, but there were other critical factors in play.

As Viktor Frankl put it in his groundbreaking 1946 book, *Man's Search for Meaning*, "Everything can be taken from a man but one thing: the last of the human freedoms—to choose one's attitude in any given set of circumstances, to choose one's own way."

Frankl (1905–1997) was a Holocaust survivor imprisoned in Nazi concentration camps, including Auschwitz and Dachau. After the war, he became a prominent Austrian philosopher, neurologist, and psychologist, sharing the profound techniques he developed to survive concentration camps.

To become a "Survivor" with the capital "S" means developing a mindset—a mental framework of beliefs and attitudes to overcome even the most challenging circumstances. But, as Frankl wrote, true survival requires more than simply not dying. It means not succumbing to grief and despair, but instead finding meaning—even looking for moments of joy—in all of life's circumstances, including the most excruciatingly painful and unjust.

Everyone, at some point in their lives, endures trauma and loss. When you come out the other side—when you "survive"—how will the experience change you? Surely the loss of loved ones transforms our lives, but it's what we do next that matters.

To me, this marks the difference between someone who breaks—paralyzed amid unwanted memories, dreams, and flashbacks—and the fierce but quiet determination of that single mother in Queens, defiantly forging the best life possible for her son, in spite of outrageous misfortune.

After the unspeakable loss of family, place, and country, my mother and her siblings had to move on to survive. But as Survivors, they did much more. They rebuilt their lives, created new families, and found varying degrees of meaning, happiness, and joy.

To me, that's the crux of post-traumatic growth. After having sufficient time to process and mourn your life's events—can you rise again, above the shadows and back into the light? Can you, like Frankl, find new meaning and joy in living despite the grief and horrors?

Fighting cancer is no different. I can't change the facts surrounding my brain tumor nor direct its course. I can only change my attitudes and beliefs about how I choose to live my life.

It's a well-known adage that "if life gives you lemons, make lemonade." Nobody I know exemplified this sentiment better than my mother. No amount of suffering could embitter a woman of such strength and love. Overcoming the horrors of her youth nearly perishing in Auschwitz, moving to a foreign continent all alone, then facing battles with cancer and the loss of her husband, my mother—the resilient Survivor, Susan Cooper—squeezed every ounce of happiness from her life.

As my distant cousin, the novelist Elie Wiesel, once said, "There is divine beauty in learning...To learn means to accept the postulate that life did not begin at my birth. Others have been here before me, and I walk in their footsteps."

I grew up watching my mother's strength of mind and character. I always admired how she took care of me without sacrificing too much for herself. Susan Cooper did things her own way—and when I finally came of age to set out on my own, I was determined to do the same. To honor those that came before, and every step they took.

Chapter 5
Starting From Scratch

August 27, 1979: My first day of college

I arrived at Vassar's campus in Poughkeepsie, New York, for early pre-orientation—eager to get in before the rush and start the rest of my life.

Some kids go to college to grow up, some go to party, and others go to find themselves. I still had some growing up to do, but I think of my college days as my coming out party of who I already was.

In addition to the "Cooper Rule" of decisive forward movement, childhood taught me not to worry much about the labels or expectations other people put on me. This would come in handy through college and into my entrepreneurial career. Over the course of my life, I'd go on to be labeled both a success and a failure—not to mention, arrogant, aggressive, impatient, and a smart ass. But like my mother before, I learned to follow my instincts, remember who I am, and build my own life.

At seventeen years old—the same age my mother was when she survived Auschwitz and bravely set out on her own—I was finally free to explore and stretch the edges of my comfort zone. College provided the freedom to study new topics and hear different points of view from students of different backgrounds. Plus, there was much more time in the day to do whatever I chose.

To start my college career and forge my own life—completely from scratch.

When I entered my dorm room for the first time, it took only ten minutes to meet my first college friend and get pinned with a nickname for life.

Joel—who went by "JB"—from Rockaway, Queens, shouted out to me from the hallway,

"Yo, Lex!" Just like that, I had my college persona.

Even during my first days on campus, Vassar fit like an old pair of leather penny loafers. I learned the school offered more than just a favorable ratio of women to men. I'd finally found my melting pot of cultures, ethnicities, and ideas. Despite our eclectic backgrounds, there was a common bond among the first co-educational classes at Vassar. We all wanted a different college experience where it was safe to explore who we were without judgment.

The autonomy and responsibility I'd carried in childhood endowed me with a sense of maturity, so part of doing things *my* way meant staying within self-imposed boundaries. Used to making my own decisions, I felt fully in command of my life. I had no problems choosing my classes or major, what crowd I wanted to hang out with, whether to do drugs, or how much to drink.

Vassar was full of smart kids, so I had to work hard. I was determined to earn honors, using my college experience to propel me forward. But it wasn't all work and no play. Even my mother also had her guilty pleasures, occasionally leaving me for an evening to go to the horse races or Atlantic City. She'd taught me that it's okay to let loose a little—within reason. There were certain lines I would not cross.

I felt beholden to my mother's sacrifices and expectations and tethered to my survivor instincts to not overdo it. Besides, I lacked the discretionary funds for ski trips and beach vacations. Unlike most other students, I had to work during school breaks and summer vacations. I wasn't jealous though. I no longer felt like an outsider or feared missing out.

I did at least make it a couple of times to Fort Lauderdale for spring break—in an old, beat-up Toyota with a few college buddies. I even found gainful employment there, getting paid for running fun promotions on the beach.

The college experiences that most shaped my future came from sources outside the standard Vassar course catalog or list of extracurricular activities. I didn't just want to just join something, I wanted to come together with my peers and build something entirely new.

This impulse would serve as a precursor for my entrepreneurial days to come. But for now, I'd apply it to my first love: baseball.

Let's Play Ball

One of the historical "Seven Sisters" women-only colleges, Vassar became co-ed in 1969. Still, men's varsity sports remained limited by my arrival. In the mid-70s, school colors changed from pink to maroon and gray (to better attract male athletes), and the school mascot switched from "Big Pink" to the Brewers, in honor of Matthew Vassar, who'd made his fortune brewing beer.

During my first semester at Vassar, I found a notice in the student center. Upperclassmen were recruiting guys for a newly formed club-level men's baseball team. I signed up without hesitation or expectations—which is good, because we were a ragtag bunch, lacking a coach, ballfield, equipment, and uniforms.

We didn't care. Vassar's inaugural baseball team immediately bonded over a shared love for the game and the idealistic belief that anything was possible—including founding the first-ever men's baseball program at a former women-only college. We had to pick rocks off the field, mow the grass, and line the base paths ourselves. We wore old used warm-up jackets from the former men's basketball team. We didn't even have numbers on these makeshift uniforms.

But in every respect, we were a team. We practiced in the gym during winters, constructed a batting cage with a pitching machine next to the old bowling alley in the basement, played in snow during bitter conditions, and endured long bus rides and even longer double-header losses by opponents that overmatched our meager squad.

I recall one early loss against the West Point Military Academy JV team. At some point—mid-inning—we were up to bat when we heard a cannon blast over the Hudson. To the left of our dugout, next to a waving American flag, a bugler began playing taps, and all the West Point cadets, both on the field and in the dugout, stopped what they were doing to stand at attention, with their hats over their hearts.

Meanwhile, we morons had no clue what was happening. Most of us were goofing around in our hand-me-down uniforms, laughing, when someone from the cadet side stuck his head into our dugout and bellowed like a drill sergeant: "Shut up, take off your hats, and salute the flag!"

The inaugural Brewers team only played ten games our first year, and our record was 1-9—one win and nine losses.

It didn't matter. We had camaraderie, a modest but loyal fan base, and the usual rookie hazing, including the time I somehow forced myself to swallow the two-inch, segmented mezcal worm at the bottom of our tequila bottle. By our second year, we even had a coach, Dan Gordon, plus new shirts with ironed-on numbers.

I've joined teams and clubs to play sports and socialize my entire life. Leagues and groups came and went, but playing college baseball at Vassar during my freshman year remains my top team sports experience. We'd built something bigger than the sum of all the walks, hits, outs, and runs scored on the field. We were pioneers, leaving our legacy of a thriving varsity men's baseball program for more than thirty-five years to come.

Computers and Cognitive Science

College offered another chance to forge something new. This was the early days of personal computers, and I was fascinated. I'd been lucky enough to get exposure to computers and basic programming in high school, and once I got to Vassar, I signed up for every computer science class I could. Unfortunately, I couldn't yet major in the field—it was considered a vocational subject, like accounting, and therefore not worthy of a well-rounded liberal arts bachelor's degree.

In addition to my love for computers, I discovered courses in the then-new field of "cognitive science." Cognitive science spanned psychology, linguistics, neuroscience, philosophy, and computer science—and while I was there, Vassar began offering one of the nation's first undergraduate cognitive science disciplinary programs.

I had found my major. I also, along with my friend, Gard, found a way to convert my love for computers into service when we both began to teach computer skills to kids in a program that was run by Columbia University.

I've always loved exploring the big questions of cognitive science: how do humans think? How does the brain store and retrieve information? What is the nature of human cognition, and can computers become sentient?

Forty years later, we still struggle to answer these questions. One of the basic principles of early cognitive science research was that human memory, reasoning, language, and problem-solving would lead us to build computer models and software to replicate these functions. Of course, I didn't know then that it would take two more decades to develop the computing power necessary to significantly bridge connections between human and artificial intelligence.

Meanwhile, I always worked to pay my out-of-pocket living expenses. I'd landed a part-time job at the end of high school in the data processing department at Warner Communications' swank headquarters at 75 Rockefeller Plaza in Manhattan. I kept working there into college, learning rudimentary programming in Cobol, a Mainframe programming language popular in the 1960s and '70s.

I also learned that sitting all day in a smoke-filled room of programmers, staring at a black screen and green blinking cursor on an IBM terminal was *not* my idea of intellectually stimulating work. But the salary was good. Plus, I had a foot in the door to a lifelong career.

By 1982, the summer before my senior year, I'd grown deadly bored with the cushy job. It was time to hit the streets and find something new. That same year, the first IBM personal computer was released. I just walked into the Computerland store on 6th Avenue and 43rd Street—without a resume or scheduled interview—and asked for a job.

Before they could give me the bum's rush and kick me out to the street, I announced I would work for commission only; they had nothing to lose. In two months that summer, I made over $5,000 in commissions, winning a sales contest, along with the first IBM personal computer to grace Vassar's campus—which I immediately sold to my roommate, Gard, to help me pay out-of-pocket living expenses.

From my Computerland job, I learned two valuable lessons. First, I discovered that selling is a meritocracy; you get paid for what you produce. Lesson number two was the realization that I wanted to be something more than a glorified shoe salesman—which is exactly what selling computer hardware felt like. Hardware consists of so many boxes of different sizes and specifications. I was more interested in software and applications. That, I determined, was where I would focus my career.

ELIZA

One memorable college project combined my two passions of computer science and human cognition. Our assignment? Build a chatbot psychotherapist.

While that's an oversimplification, the ELIZA programs each student built used an early form of natural language processing created in the mid-1960s by MIT professor Joseph Weizenbaum. Weizenbaum designed ELIZA to simulate the dialogue of a certain kind of clinical psychotherapist—the kind who asks questions but rarely provides answers.

Even though ELIZA was not what we consider a "learning machine," and therefore not a precursor to artificial intelligence, it still managed to reliably fool its subjects into thinking they were chatting with a human. Subjects would sit in a separate room and type responses—to either ELIZA or a human—on a keyboard. ELIZA would issue automated responses printed on the two-way teletype machine. If the "patient" could not reliably tell whether the responses came from a machine or a human, ELIZA passed, what's called, the Turing Test.

I'm writing this within months of Open AI releasing Chat GPT to the public. Since then, applications, advancements, and debates about artificial intelligence are popping up everywhere. Who knows? Maybe someday, AI robots will conduct or assist with brain surgeries like the ones my surgical team now performs. Artificial intelligence is already used by some surgeons to help diagnose tumors and distinguish cancerous cells from healthy tissue, and robotics already assists with certain surgical procedures.

Although almost any technology comes with intended or unintended negative consequences, I tend to remain optimistic about such advancements. Neither fearful nor suspicious of progress, I believe we have the ability to control and leverage AI for the better.

When I first started in the field of computer science, it was not yet the age of personal computers. Still, I got the sense that computers would go on to change everything, and I wanted to be a part of that. The idea of writing code and creating new software programs, especially, appealed to me. I didn't know, at the time that, while my career would remain on the forefront of computer technology, I would soon move past programming and into sales and leadership roles.

Either way, I was grateful for the chance to study and experiment with computer and cognitive science while both fields—like me—were just starting out. To me, nothing was as energizing as getting in on the "ground floor" and building toward the next big thing.

Endings and Beginnings

My final semester of college dovetailed with the continuation of a saga. While I'd been making my way at Vassar—founding baseball teams and creating ELIZA chatbot therapists—my mother's breast cancer had quietly returned and metastasized on her spine.

After hearing the news, I jumped on a train and went home to be with her. Twice, the surgeons at Memorial Sloan Kettering Hospital prepped my mother for surgery—only to cancel at the last minute. It was a dangerous operation, with a strong probability of causing more harm than good, and her oncologist and surgeon disagreed on the best course of treatment.

As she deliberated over this life-changing choice, I had to decide whether or not to return for my last couple months of school, finish my senior thesis, and graduate with my class. Mom wanted me to stay and take a leave of absence, but I made the difficult decision to return to school. I knew she had the support of close family members and friends to see her through this difficult period. It wasn't easy, but she understood my reasons.

In the end, my mother chose the more conservative treatment approach of chemotherapy without surgery. Thankfully, this proved to be the right decision, as she beat back her cancer again and even went on to live nearly fifteen more years.

Time and again, I watched Susan Cooper take command over her life and medical care and push her caregivers for answers. She put her faith in the medical establishment by finding doctors and hospitals she trusted. Still, she had to weigh each important step and make each call herself, which sometimes meant disagreeing with the diagnosis or course of treatment. I also witnessed her raw grit and stoicism, including the time I watched her calmly endure an unmedicated spinal tap without complaint.

Like me, Susan Cooper refused to be a victim or a passenger in her own life. My mother lived her life her own way, showing me how to take command of my destiny and never let circumstances or others dictate my life's course.

Welcome to the Big Time

One thing's for sure: cancer or not, she wasn't going to miss her son's graduation ceremony. Neither, for that matter, would my childhood best friend, Steve, who sat next to her in the audience.

I still remember that beautiful (if unseasonably hot) day in May. I felt a rush of pride mixed with humility as I stood sweating in my cap and gown, one foot in the past—as the child of survivors, I was the first in my family to earn a university degree—and one foot in the future I was yet to create.

Marking a Vassar tradition from the 1800s, select sophomore women, affectionately called "daisies," assembled and carried a 150-foot daisy chain down the aisles while wearing matching white dresses. Meanwhile, the sophomore male "daisies" wore blue pants and blazers with daisy print ties, passing out programs. Interrupting this noble, floral tradition, came some classic comic relief as a friend of mine received a delivery of his favorite sub sandwich as he stood in line awaiting his diploma.

We were treated to a keynote speech by the illustrious actress and Vassar alum, Meryl Streep. I still remember how one of my friends, after making his way across the stage, shaking hands with school officials, surprised everyone—and especially Ms. Streep—by planting a big, wet kiss on the celebrity's cheek.

Like my mom, Streep maintained composure and humor despite the good-natured hijinks of my classmates and friends. She ended her speech that day with a reference to the perennial choice "between the devil and the dream," which arises every day "in different little disguises."

This dilemma she referenced would be different for each person. Maybe we'd face choices that would challenge our ethics and values, or perhaps a temptation to take the "easier" route and give up on our highest aspirations.

"My advice is to look the dilemma in the face and decide what you can live with," Streep offered that day. "If you can live with the devil, Vassar hasn't sunk her teeth into your leg the way she did mine. But that conscience, that consciousness of quality, and the need to demand it can galvanize your energies, not just in your work, but in a rigorous exercise of mind and heart in every aspect of your life."

Her closing lines exemplified how I wanted to lead my life: tirelessly advancing, determined to fulfill my potential, build my own fortune, and keep pushing —one more stroke, pedal, or step forward in every race I've run. A life true to my conscience and reflecting my individual spirit, just like my mother and the generations of survivors that came before.

"Integrate what you believe into every single area of your life. Take your heart to work, and ask the most and best of everybody else too," she said, before closing with: "Good luck, and welcome to the Big Time."

SECOND LEG:
Repairs, Recalibrations and Fortune

Chapter 6
Stay in the Moment

January 31, 2023: My first surgery

The morning of my surgery, rather than heading out for a customary morning cycling session, I got wheeled into an operating room for the first time in my life. In fact, until that point, I'd never spent even a single night in a hospital since my birth—but if I had, I still wouldn't have known what to expect.

Later on, friends and family asked if I was scared—and I honestly had to think about it before answering, "No."

Three factors kept my pre-op anxiety level low. First: my complete trust in the surgical team. Second: the confidence that my physical and mental strength would contribute to a positive outcome. Third: my well-practiced mindset to focus on the present moment.

If I couldn't be pedaling over Denver hillsides that morning, I could at least channel that same grounded, single-minded focus I always manage to find while cycling—

whether the grueling and crowded 112 miles of an Ironman second leg or the quiet calm of a solo morning ride.

This brings us to another principle I attribute to my IronCEO Mindset: *Stay in the moment.*

It's easy to get overwhelmed when thinking about all the risks and implications of life-changing events—especially when they come on fast and threaten everything you've known. As I prepared for surgery, overwhelm wasn't an option; I needed to be strong for my wife and children.

To help with that, I added a mindfulness meditation practice to my pre-op regimen. It's something I had tried on and off—but to be honest, I would have much rather been climbing slopes on my bike than just sitting around watching myself breathe. The focused flow state that accompanies intense physical activity had always been my meditation—and medication—of choice. However, going into surgery, I needed to find new methods for staying in the moment. Ones that didn't involve entrepreneurial drive or extreme athletic competition.

Regardless of what would happen in that operating room and afterward, I wanted to demonstrate strength in this perilous moment and radiate the same to my loved ones as they endured the agony of waiting for updates.

We would all need courage and resilience that day, and in the weeks and months ahead, so I proceeded the best way I knew how: one moment at a time.

Operating Theater

The day of the surgery moved quickly, like everything else in the past month. I arrived in the waiting room at 10 a.m. with my wife and our blended family of four now-grown kids, who had all flown in. By 11:30 a.m., I had my final blood work, blood pressure check, and the IV line put in. Beth and my daughter, Jess, sat beside me as I lay on a gurney in a pre-op waiting area.

Finally, it was time to enter the operating theater. Having never been in one before, I had no expectations. But I knew I needed to get into what athletes sometimes called a "flow state." I blocked out any thoughts or feelings not relevant or helpful to the present situation: a brightly lit, sterile room with swiftly moving clinicians, presently clamping the right side of my head and cheek into place.

It was showtime, and my brain was the main attraction.

Luckily, before the first sedatives kicked in, I didn't have much time to think. That would change when they woke me up after the first forty-five minutes.

As I dozed face up on the operating table, the surgical team performed the craniotomy, cutting out a chunk of my skull to expose my brain. Then, as promised, the anesthesiologist woke me up.

For the next three hours, I would be conscious and alert as the surgeon and speech therapist tested my brain to carefully remove cancerous tissue without disturbing critical brain functions.

Those interactions with the speech therapist were a godsend and the most memorable part of the surgery. Having already mapped the functional landscape of my brain with the earlier MRI, the surgeon wanted to test and confirm this brain map. They did so by literally poking parts of my brain while the speech therapist held up a tablet-sized screen and asked me to read sentences similar to the ones I'd been shown during the MRI. Other times she'd have me count fingers or answer questions like, "Do you feel any sensations in your body right now?"

I never felt any pain (although I do remember the odd tingling in my hand and other extremities while they were testing this brain function). Aside from the additional, slight discomfort of having my head and neck clamped down, the whole thing reminded me a little of dental surgery, where—at worst—you feel strange but tolerable pressure, this time on my skull rather than my jaw.

During those four and a half hours, I compartmentalized the risks and possible outcomes documented on those many consent forms, blocking them from my conscious mind. My only job was to keep breathing, remain calm and alert, and correctly answer the next question.

I later learned that, in addition to ensuring my speech centers remained intact, the speech therapist's most critical role was simply to put me at ease. Having a friendly voice to listen and talk to kept my mind off the full, harrowing reality of the situation. She'd sometimes ask questions just to distract me with conversation. Luckily, I loved to talk, so I regaled her with stories about my life—my work as a serial founder and CEO, my passion for Ironman races and for inspiring others to pursue their goals, and of course, my beloved family—who anxiously waited down the hall.

During a few tense moments, the speech therapist held my hand with a warmth and compassion I will never forget. This experience changed my perspective on surgeons and their clinical teams. I had always thought of surgeons as similar to me in the sense that I had never been overly sentimental. Still, tough and rugged IronCEO or not, this surgery exposed more than a segment of my brain, it also brought me face-to-face with my own vulnerability in a new way—forcing me to accept those human limitations and variables that no amount of positive mindset or mindfulness techniques could fully protect against.

As I lay immobilized on the operating table, I knew this was no longer about my intellectual curiosity about medical technology and neuroscience. Given the sky-high stakes, a lot could have gone wrong that day. But since none of it was within my control, I chose not to think about it.

With a medical team of surgeons, anesthesiologists, and nurses standing over me, and a speech therapist peppering me with questions, I honestly didn't have much time for thoughts to wander to bad places. This wasn't an Ironman race, where I had the luxury of time for idle daydreams while swimming, cycling, or running.

Sometimes, I've had to work hard to stay mindful and in the moment. This was not one of them.

Only later that evening—after the surgical team put Humpty Dumpty's head back together and wheeled my gurney into the post-op recovery area in the ICU, did the reality that my skull had just been cracked open and a massive, deadly lump cut out begin to sink in—along with considerable anxiety.

Still unable to move from my gurney, thoughts and feelings flooded into my mind. I began wondering about my long-term prognosis and how my all-important daily training routines would change. While I felt no physical pain, it was finally sinking in that my skull had been cracked open and a clementine-sized mass cut out of my brain.

Not wanting to think any longer, I asked the anesthesiologist to put me back into a light sleep. The time for doubts and questions would come later. For now, I needed to rest.

Recovery Begins

I woke up in the post-op area approximately thirty minutes after the surgery ended. I was allowed two visitors, so Beth and my son, Evan, quickly joined me at my bedside before we could reunite with Jess, Molly, and Ben. After hours in the dark, waiting for updates on my surgery, I could see the relief in my family's eyes as they saw me in command of my mental faculties, cracking jokes and giving hugs.

The surgeon's initial post-op feedback was very positive. He'd been able to remove more than 90 percent of the tumor—a great outcome. Still, it was a lot to process. I felt relieved and happy to get through the experience without any short-term ramifications, but I knew I was facing a long, uncertain road ahead.

True to the surgeon's words, I'd woken up without feeling groggy or nauseous. Miraculously, I felt a little discomfort after the surgery. While required to spend two nights in the ICU and offered all kinds of potent but addictive pain meds, I'd accept only Tylenol to treat my mild headache. My decision to stay awake and take minimum anesthesia was already paying off. To my triathlon-obsessed brain, recovery had already begun.

It's over, I thought. *Time to get back to living!*

I didn't yet know what that meant, but I was ready to put in the work to find out. While I expected my physical fitness to aid recovery from surgery, chemotherapy, and radiation treatments, I knew that my mental fitness—my IronCEO mindset—would ultimately count much more in terms of both recovery and basic quality of life.

During those days in the ICU, nurses periodically checked my vitals and did blood work. With my resting heart rate under 50, blood oxygen over 96, and the blood pressure of a thirty-year-old, I was the least of their concerns.

During the next phase of my recovery, I faced no new physical challenges. Still, I was disappointed to discover I still had issues coordinating basic movements and perceiving the positions of my right arm and hand. Still, the greatest impediments to recovery would be emotional, mental, and cognitive. I had to buffer my boundless determination, impatience, and expectations.

Luckily, I've always been able to improvise and adjust course. While many of my fellow Ironman triathletes swear by rigid, disciplined training regimens, I've always been more of a flow guy, responding and adapting to life's major plot twists. Chalk it up to survivor mentality, staying in the moment, or my desire to get ahead of the next new thing—I don't tend to wallow in worry or indulge in self-pity. One thing

I would have to learn, however, is to accept new limitations and even the frustrations that sometimes accompany those.

Calling the Shots

So much about having cancer—the diagnosis, treatment options, and prognosis—is largely out of the patient's hands. However, I could take charge of both my physical and mental recovery.

It wasn't just a matter of returning to an exercise routine. Once again, I had to own the narrative and stay grounded in each moment in order to make the most of my recovery and the precious time I had left.

In this situation (and in many), "owning the narrative" didn't mean rewriting the script. I was not here to deny reality or pretend I was not sick. But I would not let this illness dictate how I live my life. I wanted my wife, family, and friends to see me as I saw myself: the same vibrant, willful man who started three companies from nothing and recently finished his tenth Ironman race.

To the extent I could, I called my own shots and set my own pace. I could control a few things in the hospital, including what I ate and, to some extent, what medications I chose to take. It took a lot for me to lose my appetite, but I still wanted healthier fare than the prepackaged, reheated foods on offer. So, my family smuggled in some delicious treats—casual takeout lunches from my favorite market deli, along with fresh salads. I also refused to take oxycontin and all other non-essential medications. Finally, I determined how much time I spent in a hospital bed by greeting visitors from a comfortable day chair.

None of this surprised my wife and children. They knew I was going to take charge of my illness and recuperation as much as possible. I quickly tired out my physical therapist by demonstrating that I could walk around the ICU ward as many laps as she had the stamina to join me.

Before we left, my wife sternly pointed out that no one had tested my steadiness in climbing stairs, and we were about to return home to a four-story townhouse, with my bedroom on the second floor. So, before discharging me, the physical therapist returned to watch me sprint up two flights of stairs in the stairwell before flashing my signature finish-line smile.

At 1 p.m. on Wednesday, February 1—exactly two days and two hours after being admitted for surgery—I walked out of the CU Anschutz inpatient pavilion on my own two feet.

The Courage to Be Present

While happy to go home, I would not be lulled into thinking I had won the battle. My cancer could not be completely removed without risking serious damage. I may have looked good, felt strong, and carried the attitude of a man who could conquer any challenge, but I did not feel triumphant.

My family and I had to come to grips with the fact that I still had an incurable disease with an unknown life expectancy. I was honest and transparent about that from day one. That meant we would all experience the fear and grief of a terminal prognosis and the stress of uncertainty.

I may have accidentally prophesied that I would face steep new challenges after the Madison, Wisconsin, Ironman race, but I certainly did not wish this upon myself and my loved ones. There were no pretty ribbons to tie around my cancer. Beth, the kids, and I would continue to face difficult times and dark emotions along with this new reality.

Like it or not, it's all part of staying in the moment. Life throws you moments you never asked for and would love to reject or change. It takes strength and courage to stay present through discomfort, pain, and fear instead of numbing yourself with denial, false hopes, or unhealthy coping mechanisms.

Luckily, I'd already gotten plenty of practice accepting pain and exhaustion. In some ways, I've made a habit of seeking it out through grueling endurance races—not to mention the pressure and frustrations inherent in launching and running businesses.

Like most entrepreneurs, I was most comfortable when I could take charge of situations and forge ahead, but I'd also learned to discern which aspects of life I could and could not control. This applied to business, athletic training, and now, living with cancer.

I knew I couldn't directly control the disease in my body. Pathology tests confirmed the diagnosis of glioblastoma—a rare, incurable form of cancer. With surgery, radiation, and chemotherapy, the best we could aim for was to remove what they could and slow the progression. To this day, the FDA has not approved any treatments that can promise remission—let alone a cure—for this kind of cancer.

Coming out of my first surgery, this left one final question: *could I eliminate, reduce, or at least mitigate the cognitive and physical deficits caused by the tumor?*

Any hopes that the surgery might correct these issues had failed to materialize. My mobility and coordination symptoms showed no significant improvement after the surgery, nor after undergoing radiation and chemotherapy. Though frustrated by my early lack of progress, at least things weren't getting worse—an outcome I'd learn to accept as good news.

For someone who's naturally impatient and ambitious, it's hard to stay grounded in the moment when things slow down or stall out. To me, not even "immediate gratification" comes soon enough. A typical, bossy CEO, I want what I want when I want it. If I can't get it, I keep trying.

Much of the time, this impatient determination serves me well, but there have been moments when it's gotten me nowhere. Since this cancer diagnosis, I've had to learn some restraint and develop new ways of measuring "progress" or "success" in my day-to-day life.

Buddhist philosophy teaches that the future and past are illusory—that *now* is the only real moment there is. Even when that "now" feels scary, uncomfortable, or even intolerable.

As I adjusted to my new limitations, I needed to center myself—to take each moment as it came and not let fears or expectations define how I lived the rest of my life. I had no choice but to take it one moment at a time, maintaining self-trust and optimism as I went. Otherwise, I was not living; I was simply waiting to die.

My late ancestor, Elie Wiesel once wrote: "Even in darkness, it is possible to create light and encourage compassion."

Sometimes, creating that light requires effort: single-minded forward momentum toward goals or active service to others. Other times—as I've learned from the mindfulness meditation I still practice—it means settling the mind and cultivating *self*-compassion. Making the most of every moment *exactly* as it comes. Even if all you can do at that moment is close your eyes, sit still, and observe the rhythm—the tremendous gift—of each breath.

Chapter 7
"Shut Up, Legs"

September 29, 2002: The tragedy

My being and bike are bonded like fine-crafted welds on a handmade steel frame. If I had never ridden a bicycle, my life would still be wonderful, but it wouldn't be the same. The twists, turns, ups, and downs I've experienced in this life are deeply intertwined with my bicycle journey—for both good and ill.

As a central backstory to my life, cycling has enriched, empowered, and sustained me, though not without considerable struggle and grit—including an unspeakable loss that would strain my relationship with cycling and endurance sports nearly beyond repair.

Above all, the story of my life on two wheels is one of resilience. This chapter title, "Shut Up Legs," references the autobiography and catchphrase of Jens Voigt, a retired German professional cyclist, media darling, and fan favorite—whose mantra reminds me that the mind dictates what the body can do. The will to keep going, whether to cross the finish line first or simply survive grueling race conditions, can overcome and far surpass what you think you're capable of.

While racing, and in all parts of life, I was determined to never use pain, fatigue, or anything else as an excuse or distraction to keep me from fulfilling my potential. Even when I had no idea how I would finish a race or pursue a business plan, I never considered the option of giving up on a passion or goal.

Until that fateful September day—just one year and a few weeks after I stood in my office watching flames engulf the World Trade Center and twenty years before my final Ironman race. What began as an ordinary morning ride claimed the life of a woman I loved, right before my eyes, and it very nearly ended my commitment to cycling.

Until that moment, the bicycle had always been my private, sacred sanctuary. A quiet refuge from the demands of work and life, even when it strained my muscles and mind beyond all limits. I could always dig deeper and apply my survivor mentality, finding the will to push tired limbs over one more hill and past the next milepost...and then the next.

Reclaiming this area of my life required new levels of resilience. The ability to reconcile grief with the indomitable spirit is modeled by the likes of Jens Voigt. Getting back on the bike saddle would prove one of the more difficult—and defining—decisions I've made. One I had to do alone.

Speaking of lone efforts, Voigt often launched ill-advised solo attacks long distances from the finish line. In a race, "solo attack" describes the bold move of breaking away from the peloton (a large group of riders) and riding alone. To gain an advantage in this way, riders must maintain pacing against much greater wind resistance.

Some journeys in life require breaking away from the pack and defiantly setting off on your own. I knew from my survivor roots that when tragedy threatens to break your spirit, that is the most important time to push through. To keep pedaling through the pain. To get up when you fall and get back in the race, even—especially—when you most feel like giving up.

That's the measure of true resilience.

Early Misadventures

When you're old enough to drive a car or take a train, the utility of bike riding takes a backseat. Later, some of us find a reason to return to the childlike joy of riding, whether for recreation, transportation, or serious sport. Others move on, leaving their bikes to sit in a garage, collecting rust and dust.

Still, those early memories remain etched in our minds. Especially for kids of my generation, that first bicycle meant freedom. Even in an urban environment like New York City, getting a bike opened my horizons, allowing me to explore my world without relying on an adult to get around.

I learned to ride a bike on the corner of 68th Drive and Yellowstone Avenue in Forest Hills, Queens, in front of my best friend Steve's apartment building. With my mother at work and no father or sibling to show me how to ride, Steve was my teacher.

I lived halfway up the block, but our lessons took place at the bottom, by necessity. The hill between Queens Boulevard and Yellowstone Avenue was way too steep for a beginner to dare an attempt. (Ten years later, after buying my first car, I would forget this valuable information, struggling to drive and park a manual transmission vehicle on such a steep grade.)

Innocence has its virtues, but also its vices. After only a few quick lessons, Steve shoved me onto the street and said, "Let's go!" After assuring my unknowing mother I would only ride on the sidewalks, we took to the streets of Forest Hills and beyond.

When I grew up, no helicopter parents monitored our activities. So, we soon went looking for the fastest, steepest hills to race and new terrains to explore. While only eight miles from our Forest Hills block to Manhattan, the ride seemed like 50 to two Queens kids.

Luckily, it was a simple route. We made a right turn on Queens Boulevard and headed due west for eight miles. Then, we rode over the service lane on the 59th Street Bridge (now the Ed Koch Bridge), "feeling groovy" like the Simon and Garfunkel song named for the landmark overpass. Finally, we cycled from First to Fifth Avenue and straight into Central Park.

Back then, the service road over the bridge was a metal grate, unpaved and barely wide enough for the one-way car traffic that buzzed by as we rode over the East River. Years later, New York City finally paved the road and restricted it to pedestrian use only. Back then, we were two oblivious kids from Forest Hills, unaware that Queens Boulevard had earned a grim and well-deserved nickname that still applies: the "Boulevard of Death."

Between 1990 and 2017, at least 186 people, mainly pedestrians, had died in collisions on this infamous stretch of road. I found this statistic on a New York City-based law firm's personal injury case website. Need I say more?

At thirteen, we used bar mitzvah money to buy our first 10-speeds. Steve invested in a fancy Peugeot racing import, and I got a vintage Royce Union Road bike. I felt like royalty on the road—at least, for the few weeks it lasted.

We fixed a new destination in our sights: the Kissena Velodrome. This 400-meter banked oval cycling race track still ranks among New York City's best-kept secrets. Known in the cycling community as the "track of dreams," it certainly felt less ominous than the "Boulevard of Death."

Without the assistance of modern GPS, we navigated numerous Queens neighborhoods to reach our destination.

Once the track finally came into view, it seemed like the world's seventh wonder. Originally, built for the 1964 Olympic Trials, the patchwork and bumpy track showed its age but didn't diminish its glory.

Steve and I cycled a few laps around the track, barely leaving the safety of the flat lower lanes of the track. Eventually, we stopped to take a break, sitting down in the empty bleachers.

Before long, a couple of kids about our age sat beside us.

"Hey, nice bikes!" they said, amicably, followed up with: "Mind if we borrow them for a quick lap?"

We proudly—foolishly—agreed to let these friendly new acquaintances experience the joy of flying around the banked oval track in our new 10-speeds—momentarily forgetting that the word "borrow" holds specific connotations in mid-century Queens: *taking and not giving back*.

After a quick lap, the two boys headed straight for the exits with our bikes, never to be seen again. Luckily, we'd held onto enough pocket change for a bus ride home, along with an invaluable life lesson straight from the streets of New York.

Building a Life

After high school, cycling took a hiatus through college and into my earliest years of launching a career. It seemed there was no need, no time, and no place for bike riding past boyhood adventures.

Besides Central Park, New York City in the 1970s and early '80s offered no trails for two-wheeled, leg-powered machines. As such, cycling represented a true counterculture, populated by either foolhardy kids or serious racers. I'd outgrown the first category and hadn't yet earned entry to the second.

At the time, I was focused on becoming an entrepreneur—as well as a husband, and eventually, a father. I met my first wife during my junior year at Vassar through mutual friends. We married in 1985.

Two years later, we moved to Northern New Jersey, where one day, I happened to borrow my brother-in-law's bicycle for a quick road ride. That first trip took me seven miles north from Fort Lee to Alpine and seven miles back on the popular biking route, 9W. *Wow,* I remember thinking: *Fourteen miles—what a feat of endurance!*

Of course, at the time, I had no idea I'd go on to compete in 112-mile rides sandwiched between a nearly two-and-a-half-mile swim and a literal marathon.

Distance is a relative experience for cyclists. For a non-cyclist or casual rider, ten or twenty miles can seem exceedingly long. The rabid roadie who rides five or more days a week refers to such rides as "ATB," or a quick jaunt "around the block." Gradually, I would gain stamina and speed, but at that point, I was not yet bona fide.

Mainly, I was just trying to get the hang of early parenthood. We welcomed Evan into the world in 1990 and Jess in 1992. Despite my lack of a father figure coming up, I was amazed at how natural fatherhood felt.

One scene from fatherhood I'll always cherish, of course, was the first time I taught a child of my own how to ride a bike. Since I didn't have a father to teach me (and my mother, by necessity, worked non-stop), it felt especially poignant to impart this lifelong love to both my son and daughter—but I will never forget when Evan first ditched the training wheels. The elation of seeing him pedal unencumbered down the street was soon replaced with fear and dread as he wobbled, fell over, and crashed—hard.

But then...the boy got up, brushed himself off, and hopped right back on the saddle. This wasn't the first time Evan proved he had no quit in him—and it certainly wouldn't be the last, as he went on to become first a competitive cyclist, and then a lifelong runner.

As Albert Einstein once said, "Life is like riding a bicycle. To keep your balance, you must keep moving." Like all of life's challenges, starting and supporting a family means trusting yourself to bravely push forward and keep everything steady.

When Evan came along, followed soon after by his sister, Jess, I had plenty to balance. I was busy seeking my fortune—building my career my way in the computer industry—one that, like me, felt young, spirited, and brimming with promise and potential.

Community Rides and Races

Three things happened between my late twenties and late thirties that planted seeds for my lifelong love affair with biking. Let's start with the first two: my first triathlon and my first charity bike ride.

A college buddy living in the area had started doing triathlons and asked me to join. Our first race together was an Olympic distance event in Westchester, New York, in either 1988 or 1989. At the time, I owned a simple road bike with clip-on aerobars. I didn't even have a wet suit to brave the cold but calm waters of the Long Island Sound.

Since I didn't know what to expect, I approached this first race with a spirit of curiosity, looking for a well-rounded physical feat to test my mettle. Enduring a 1500-meter swim (just under a mile), a twenty-five-mile bike ride and a ten-kilometer run proved to be a fun challenge, but truly getting hooked would take a few more years.

Around that same time, I found out about a charity bike ride called The GWB Challenge, a reference to the George Washington Bridge, that The American Cancer Society organized annually to raise funds and awareness for cancer research. This cause naturally got my attention, considering my mother's recurring battle with cancer.

While I completed that first race to honor my mother's ongoing struggle and my father's memory, I also wanted to challenge myself to ride the longest distance offered by the event. The race took a hilly sixty-three-mile route through Northern New Jersey and the southern tip of New York State in Rockland County.

For the GWB Challenge, organizers blocked traffic on the lower level of the George Washington Bridge—spanning the Hudson River between New York City and Fort Lee, New Jersey. As the world's busiest traffic bridge, it was a special thrill to ride it without cars.

I completed my first GWB Challenge in 1989, and I still have all the event t-shirts to prove I did the ride for twenty consecutive years. It motivated me to train for longer rides and helped shift my mindset from an impulsive, adventurous "seat-of-my-pants" kind of guy to one who deeply understood the power of focus, consistency, and sheer grit.

It also changed the course of my children's lives and created an unbreakable connection between us. Every year, the long course for the GWB Challenge passed right through our neighborhood in northern New Jersey, just blocks from our house. Once they were old enough, Evan and Jess waited excitedly to see me pass through and cheer me on. But like their dad, the Cooper kids proved to be more than mere spectators—too impatient and ambitious to wait on the sidelines for long.

So, in 2002, the thirteenth year of the ride, Evan—then twelve years old—decided he wanted to join me. I registered him for the shorter distance course. Though much less grueling than the full distance, this shorter event offered the same excitement of riding with hundreds of participants across the George Washington Bridge, followed by a steep climb up the Alpine Boat Basin in New Jersey.

I've climbed that slope at least a hundred times, and even now, it remains a serious challenge. I begged my son to get off his 18-inch wheeled kids' mountain bike and walk it up the steepest sections. Evan flat-out refused—head down and fiercely (if slowly) pedaled his way up that steep incline. This determination and willpower would portend later athletic prowess.

In later years, my son and daughter would both go on to complete the full 63-mile ride, dragging their old man along with ease and grace. We all got hooked on this beautiful sport that would give us so much in the way of community, physical challenge, and personal glory—not to mention a lifestyle and life skills beyond anything we could learn from team sports alone.

Finally, the experience provided me with something every parent craves: the opportunity to spend many hours alone with their kids, away from the distractions of life, engaged in the pure joy of the ride.

In addition to memories, I have a cherished keepsake from those years: a quilt stitched from old t-shirts from each year's race. I remember the year they put that quilt up for the GWB Challenge annual raffle. After seeing the handmade collector's item on display, I put in my ticket—somehow 100 percent sure I would win it.

I was right. That quilt now hangs in my garage, right above the stationary trainer where I do my daily winter rides. This adds a homey touch to my "Pain Cave," as my fellow maniacal cyclists and I affectionately call our indoor training spaces.

This fluke of uncanny luck and keen judgment certainly didn't apply to everything in life. I made my share of mistakes in my early career and family life—but through it all, I'm grateful I reconnected with my childhood love of cycling.

Like this cozy souvenir, my love of cycling knit together decades of quality time with Evan and Jess—first watching as they enthusiastically cheered me on, then riding alongside them both in our shared, lifelong passion. It's been years since both of my children surpassed their old man in speed and endurance, continuing the legacy of resilience that began the first day their father crossed the East River on two wheels.

Road Dawgs

The third factor solidifying my cycling credentials arrived in my mid-thirties. I discovered a local cycling club called Road Dawgs. At the time, I'd done community rides and races but didn't know many techniques to improve my amateur pacing. Road Dawgs offered the perfect balance of a social riding group and competitive training from some serious hammerheads.

From the start, I enjoyed the camaraderie and challenge of riding longer and harder with the Road Dawgs but building the stamina, strength, and skill to truly keep pace would take a while. After a few years, when I could finally keep up with the pack, I even tried my hand at bike racing—and quickly discovered I was out of my league.

No problem. Road Dawgs was always more about keeping company and supporting each other than about racing.

In the summertime, we did a fast group ride every Tuesday morning. We dubbed this weekly ride "the Mambo," because it simulated an intricate, well-choreographed dance performed by a pack of cyclists riding in a peloton. In any amateur or professional level race, you'll notice cyclists lined up behind each other, with just six to 18 inches separating the lead rider's rear wheel from the front wheel behind. This seemingly death-defying feat helps riders achieve the aerodynamic benefits of drafting.

Here's how it works: the rider in front keeps nose to the wind—and uses at least 30 percent more energy to achieve the same speed as riders drafting off their back wheel. In practical terms, if I typically average just seventeen miles per hour on a flat grade, I can still draft a rider going twenty mph with no problem keeping up. Because the rider in front works so much harder, the only way to keep up the group speed is to form a rotating paceline, with each cyclist taking a turn at the front.

Depending on the fitness and power of each cyclist, the lead rider will spend between five seconds to a few minutes in front, before moving quickly to the left. As each rider carefully drifts back to the end of the queue, the next rider moves to the tip of the spear, breaking the wind for everyone else.

This takes time and skill to master, but before long, we become a well-oiled speed machine, even with a newbie on board. The trick is to avoid surging when you become the new lead but to instead allow the momentum of your drafted pace to propel you forward as long as you can. The speed of the pace line is exhilarating, especially at first. We regularly ended our twenty-mile ride, averaging over twenty miles an hour.

It took me almost a year to master the Mambo pace line and hang on for the entire twenty miles. Once I finally achieved this goal, I noticed another happy side effect of my efforts. My brain, figuratively speaking, had caught fire. Both my concentration and creativity levels were flying off the charts.

The Power of Focus

I also began to notice a powerful phenomenon when I rode hard by myself: I would spend long moments thinking about...nothing at all. This was quite the novelty for a scatterbrained thinker like me. Other times, I would surge into hyperdrive, devising creative solutions to the day's thorny work problems. I discovered I always felt more productive on work days following a rigorous morning ride.

I've never been formally diagnosed with Attention Deficit (Hyperactivity) Disorder; that wasn't a thing when I was young. But like many other high-energy entrepreneurs and creative types, I knew that sometimes I could hyper-focus with no problems. Other times, I struggled to pay attention and keep track of it all. Once I realized the mental and professional benefits of cycling, my daily exercise became non-negotiable.

Years later, I read an article in a popular bicycling magazine about a father whose child had been diagnosed with ADHD—only to discover that cycling helped reduce and manage symptoms of inattention and hyperactivity. This settled the matter: cycling would always be my drug of choice when it came to self-medicating my attention issues. I'm not trying to imply that I've heroically overcome a serious learning disorder. My academic and business accomplishments attest that I've always been highly functioning. Still, both common sense and various medical studies confirm the positive impact that regular exercise can have on the brain.

This proves especially true as our digital age keeps speeding up time, with compounding levels of distraction. The internet, smartphones, and 24-hour news cycles drive us to think that the more emails we answer, the more news stories in our feed, and the more social media we consume and post—the faster we'll rise to the top of our game. In truth, however, this mentality is a treadmill to nowhere, and my easily distracted brain needed to get off.

I am convinced that distance biking is the best way to slow down time and make distance disappear. The longer the route, the shorter it feels. While increasing overall fitness and endurance helps explain this effect, the true magic for making a four-hour trek feel like a one-hour "ATB" ride is pure mindset. Even at work, the clock moves faster when you're deeply engaged in challenging work.

Now try taking a long bike ride on a beautiful sun-kissed fall day. Soon enough, those minutes, hours, and miles melt away—along with the stress of day-to-day living.

When I finish a good ride, I return physically refreshed and mentally recharged. Usually, I have a few new ideas in my pocket, including answers to some pressing challenges of the day. The joy of the journey increases exponentially when I'm not in a rush to get somewhere in particular. This also provides a spiritual retreat where I can sift through emotional pain or stress.

Highs and Lows

Cycling has marked the highest mileposts in my life, as well as the lowest. Before the accident that would claim the life of someone dear to me and change my life, I experienced a minor wreck of my own. One that shook me up physically but also revealed some major, unexamined issues in my life.

Although cycling typically helped me to focus, I admittedly still let my thoughts wander at times while out on the road. During one early morning solo weekday ride, I was lost inside my head, hugging the curb along a quiet neighborhood in Nyack, New York—when I suddenly looked up to see a pickup truck parked directly in front of me.

I woke up from my zombie stupor just in time to swerve to the left, narrowly avoiding a rear-end collision—only to immediately slam into the extended driver's side view mirror as the driver sat inside, finishing his breakfast and coffee. I sheared the bracket and mirror right off the truck, startling him to attention.

Next, I wobbled, woozy and bloodied, before falling over right in front of his truck. The driver rushed to my assistance, sitting me up on the steps of a nearby deli and racing inside to fetch a bag of ice and a bottle of water. After coming to my senses, it became obvious that the deep cuts and bruises on my arm needed medical attention. My good samaritan (still hungry) truck driver threw my bike in the back of the truck and drove me to the Nyack Hospital emergency room.

The good news was that I'd suffered no broken bones, and my fancy carbon bicycle was undamaged. All I needed were twelve stitches to close the wound. The bad news was that I knew I had to reckon with some mounting spiritual wounds that had been weighing on my heart and mind, culminating in this physical crash: my first marriage was suffering.

I sometimes describe my first decade of marriage as my "unconscious years." I was obsessed with building a business, raising a family, and becoming an endurance athlete, but I did not devote sufficient time to nurturing the health of my marriage. As a result, a distance and growing discontent gnawed at us both. While I sensed that something was off, I couldn't put my finger on it. Whenever I approached my partner to express my concerns and ask if everything was okay, she'd deny or deflect.

My nature is to focus on the positive. But since I'd just narrowly avoided a serious accident, I had to confront my wife about what happened and why. After getting stitched up, I sat her down and confessed that this felt like more than just an innocent bike accident. I was depressed and ready to seek counseling. Her response was not exactly what I wanted to hear, but it confirmed my feelings.

My wife admitted that she was very unhappy in the marriage. While that wasn't great news, I'd finally confirmed the root of the problem and felt hopeful we could fix it. After many months of earnest marriage counseling and individual therapy, we learned that we were not meant for each other. Our subsequent divorce in 1998 was amicable, and I give full credit for her primary role in raising two wonderful children.

Like it or not, the universe exists in a constant state of change. Everyone has a choice: You can accept and embrace this fact, or you can play the victim when things inevitably change or end. I may not have control over every life-changing experience, but I can control how I respond to each one. It wasn't easy, but I embraced all the changes that divorce entailed. The kids and I continued to spend weekends together, alternately biking and skiing—the latter of which we learned to do together, developing into yet another shared athletic passion. Ultimately, the divorce turned out well for everyone involved: my ex-wife, me, and most importantly, our kids.

Neither this accident nor my obsession with cycling caused our divorce. However, I think of my bicycle as the constant witness to my life's ups and downs, including this pivotal family decision. Riding—and crashing—my bike that day forced me to wake up to some patterns that desperately needed to change.

Duty to Praise

Another profound transition occurred around this time: the death of my mother, Susan Cooper. In 1999, her cancer returned. Again, doctors advised against surgery, but this time, the chemo treatments were no match for the cancer's aggressive growth.

When her medical team moved her to Hospice care, I visited every day—and I still cherish those final moments of connection between my mother, who had seen, survived, and sacrificed so much for me to have the extraordinary gift of a regular American suburban life. It's easier to appreciate what you have when you've worked so hard, in the face of so many obstacles. While I understood I might be playing with a smaller deck than others in our middle-class neighborhood, I also knew that I never wanted for anything—and for that, I was grateful.

Mom and I didn't exactly share our feelings much growing up. The word "taboo" doesn't really do justice to the visceral reality of unspoken terror and grief that marked my mother's childhood and youth. Looking back, it's not so much that she didn't want me to know things but that she still felt the weight of that past she'd escaped and compartmentalized to move on.

I imagine opening that up—even just a crack—would feel like inviting a ravenous flood. She wasn't about to spoil the peace and security of the life she'd worked so hard to build for me. Those memories had no place there. Besides, the lady was tough as nails. I understood how hard she worked and why—as always, a mother's love and support. So, I quietly helped her carry that weight, a skill I mastered from watching her.

Those final talks felt different. They didn't bring some huge revelation or disclosure about the past—that wasn't necessary. In fact, I can't even recall the details of our conversations during my visits to Hospice care. But I still feel the quality of our connection. How close we felt, and how tenderly we spoke.

Susan Cooper passed away on April 10, 2000, two days after I turned 38. (I somehow knew, with quiet conviction, that she'd hold on until after my birthday, sparing me that lifelong association.) The day she died, I brought my copy of the siddur—Jewish prayer book—and read aloud the *Aleinu*. Not that I needed to read it; that prayer remained forever etched into my mind from my childhood temple days. Still, I wanted to feel the old, worn book in my hand and see those familiar words as I spoke them.

Commonly recited near the end of Jewish worship services, its name can be translated as "duty to praise," underscoring the anchor of faith despite life's trials and tragedies. Neither she nor I have ever been too religious, but those familiar Hebrew words sounded more palpable, more *real* than ever before. Aleinu still reminds me of my mother and all the wonderful gifts she gave me. I hope those words brought her the same comfort they continue to bring me.

In weeks following my mother's death, my bike rides helped me channel grief into pure physical effort, fueled by increased heart rate and heartache. Suddenly, riding along the well-known streets of my adult life brought me back to those early days, barreling down Queens Boulevard with Steve—surviving traffic by the skin of our teeth and reveling in the false indestructibility of youth.

Bicycles may be inanimate objects, but they've played leading roles in almost every aspect of my life: adding structure and focus to my impulsive tendencies, teaching me the power of resilience, and finally: serving as an unwitting catalyst to my most life-changing moments—not just the end of my first marriage, but also new loves and losses that would come in the years ahead.

Gone Too Soon

After the divorce, I eventually got back into the dating scene. In 2000, one woman reached out to me through an early dating website. To protect her family's privacy, I'll call her "Jill" rather than using her real name.

Jill sent me a long email, which I admittedly waited to respond to. I didn't mean to ignore her; I'd just been busy traveling for work and didn't see the message right away. But rather than waiting or giving up, Jill sent another message expressing her annoyance that I hadn't yet responded—mainly because she thought we had much in common and would be a great match.

Now Jill had my full attention. Someone else may have interpreted her second email as pushy desperation. But to my way of thinking, it was all *perspiration*. I know from experience that you only get what you want if you ask for it—then push hard. That, to me, seemed to be exactly what Jill was doing.

Our first date—at a pub halfway between our towns—exceeded all expectations, proving that Jill's instincts were right. We soon began seeing each other regularly. Jill was also divorced with three young children. Not only was she clearly a devoted parent, she also loved biking. Before long, we'd built a committed, loving relationship. We cycled together regularly and even began bringing the kids together to test out the dynamics of potentially blending our families and lives. Our forward momentum and compatibility energized us both, and the future felt expansive and bright.

More than a year into the relationship, I was still warming up to the idea of remarriage—but I was always ready for a bike ride. On one such ride, a beautiful crisp autumn day in 2002, I did not suspect Jill and I would spend our final moments together.

As on 9/11, just one year before, I still remember every movement and moment during the first few minutes of that short and dreadful ride.

At the time, I usually started my rides heading away from the suburban town center of my northern New Jersey town and toward the quieter roads in northwestern Bergen County. However, that day—for some inexplicable reason—we headed in the opposite direction. With Jill behind me, we rode two blocks east, then crossed the railroad tracks to a busy commercial street lined with shops and restaurants.

With just one lane of traffic in each direction and constant congestion due to parking, cars along this town center barely exceeded twenty miles per hour. I entered the main street first. When I saw a big commercial truck riding eastbound ahead of me, I quickly and instinctively hopped up on the curb to join pedestrians on the sidewalk.

Since cyclists have a legal right to the road, and suburban New Jersey traffic remains pretty light, I tended to stay on the road. However, I wasn't used to seeing such a huge vehicle in this shopping district, so something told me to take more extreme, curb-hopping measures.

I assumed Jill was right behind me and had followed me onto the sidewalk. Instead, unbeknownst to me, she'd dropped behind by a block or two. Since she didn't see my response to the truck, she chose to remain on the road. Just like she was legally permitted to do, and just as she and I had safely done, dozens and dozens of times before.

I traveled about a block down this busy downtown area, slowing down to keep pace with foot traffic. I was about to hop off and turn around to check on Jill when I heard a blood-curdling scream.

At that moment, my entire body turned to ice. I felt blood drain from my face and my body froze in place. The truck I'd taken pains to avoid had attempted to pass Jill as she hugged the curb of this narrow, busy street. It ended up striking her from behind, eliciting a scream from a horrified pedestrian who witnessed the accident.

In a daze, I found myself half-consciously power-walking my bike through a confused and noisy crowd to the accident scene. My racing mind swirled with shock—along with one single word, repeating like a flashing red light in my head until it finally reached my lips: "No, no, no, no . . ."

I had to avert my eyes from the unimaginable sight. Police quickly descended, followed by an ambulance. Paralyzed, I watched as EMTs tried to revive Jill before lifting her onto a gurney and rushing to the nearest hospital, less than a mile away.

I snapped to attention and rushed to the hospital by bike. Jill was pronounced dead soon after I arrived. She was only thirty-nine.

True Resilience

No words could sufficiently express the tragic loss of such a young woman—so full of life, with three children left behind.

But while my mind could offer no words of consolation or redemption for this heart-crushing twist of fate, it could—and immediately did—begin churning through hundreds of things I could have done differently that day. If we had only gone our usual route to quieter roads…if I'd ridden more slowly and made sure Jill followed me onto the sidewalk…even if I'd done nothing at all but leave five minutes later—I'm sure the outcome would have been different.

It's not that I blame myself. I know better than to think like that—but there's no way the heart can fully accept a preventable loss like that. There will always be a part of me that wishes and wonders how things could have worked out differently so that Jill could still be here today, with her children, living her life.

After an investigation, the police ruled Jill's death an accident, assigning no fault to the driver. The first and—until right now, the only—time I told this story in full was the day I described that morning's events in painstaking detail at the police station. Now, twenty-one years later, I tell it again as I write these words. It's the one memory I wish I could erase, forget, or alter—the single most painful and harrowing experience of my life.

Just one year before her accident, after I'd witnessed the attack on the World Trade Center, I remember the overjoyed relief in her voice when she answered my call and heard I was safe. I also remember that I'd felt strangely detached from Jill in the days following the terrorist attack. How could anyone who hadn't been there and seen those things possibly understand what I was going through?

Now, that old survivor's guilt resurfaced as I struggled through new depths of grief and regret. Not even my go-to musical salvation, Bruce Springsteen, could lift my spirits. It's not that I felt guilty for surviving either event or moving on with life, but that stubborn question quietly lingered in the background: *why not me?*

Why had I survived when others died? Why was I given this time? What was I supposed to do with it?

These close brushes with death reinforced my belief that I had some purpose to fulfill. That's not to say I thought I was exceptional or better than anyone else. However, with the survivor ethos ingrained into my life and ancestry, I must find meaning in living my life. Simply surviving was not enough.

Many things can cause us to succeed and overcome instead of succumbing to our challenges. While the circumstances we're born into remain out of our control, they can offer either privileges or disadvantages. Either way, it's on us to decide what to do with those.

I wanted to live my life as a tribute to those I never wanted to leave behind. To honor the victims of 9/11, not just through my fundraising races, but through my perseverance and grit—and by appreciating every moment I had as the incredible gift it was. I wanted to be a man Jill and my mother would have both been proud of—a man who loved his family, lived his life to the fullest, and never gave up.

After months of inexpressible grief, I knew I had to get off the couch and re-enter the world. After all, when one door closes, another one opens. The trick is to be ready when it does.

The first step, I realized, was to work up the courage to get back on my bicycle. But it felt inconceivable to return to a pastime that ended Jill's life. For many months after the accident, I could hardly look at or even *think about* riding a bike again.

Eventually, I realized how empty my life was becoming. This was more than grief for a partner gone too soon, it was also the loss of a passion I'd shared not—just with Jill, but also with my two young children. A passion that ran deeper and longer than any other interest.

To me, the humble bicycle, more than anything else in this world, represented grit and fortitude. But it also still evoked a youthful sense of freedom and possibility. Voigt felt this, too. Despite the cutthroat competition of bike racing, he never let his (very serious) will to win diminish his sense of humor—rooted in a childhood pastime that, like life itself, should always stay rooted in the joy of the ride.

Years later, I would go on to read a book by leading resilience expert Angela Duckworth called *Grit: The Power of Passion and Perseverance*. Her book title tells you all you need to know: "With grit," she writes, "you can have all the perseverance in the world, but if you don't have passion, you will not be able to achieve your goal."

Not everyone finds the kind of passion that translates into lifelong resilience and joy. I sensed this truth long before I had the language to express it. That realization led me to finally pull my bike out of the garage and get back in the saddle. In honor of those lost, I would not abandon the passion that brought so much meaning, focus, and resilience to my life.

Just as running and weight lifting build calluses on your hands and feet, I think of resilience like a mental callus, building the inner toughness you need to overcome the next obstacle. Not just to get through it but to grow stronger with each recovery from challenges, disappointments, and even trauma.

In time, resilience becomes a practice in itself, just like exercise or mindfulness meditation. The first time your leg cramps up while running, you're unsure what to do next. *Should I stop running or keep going? Did I get the cramp because of an injury, lack of hydration, or not stretching?* Even if you don't know the cause, you learn to stretch your legs, slow to a walk, and—before you know it, you're running again. Each time this happens, you find a way to keep going.

That's true resilience, born from experience and learned confidence.

Losing Jill helped teach me these lessons, including embracing potential failure as a lesson rather than hesitating from fear. If you're too scared to fail, you'll never take that first step toward an audacious goal. You'll never push yourself to new speeds or distances, and you'll never achieve new heights for yourself or those who depend on you.

In other words, you may survive, but you won't be truly living.

Eventually, I realized I needed to open my heart, as well. When friends offered to fix me up, I certainly did not expect that my first blind date after Jill's death would become the love of my life and my current wife, Beth.

At the time, I had friends who doubted my decision to get back into cycling or the dating scene. But, after what I'd gone through in my life and career, I knew better than to listen to naysayers. After all, this was my life. I knew, from both distance cycling and entrepreneurship, that I had to trust my instincts and keep pressing on—to shut out the criticism, shout "shut up, legs," and do more than survive.

It was easy to associate resilience with a determined entrepreneur who refused to quit. Even better: an indomitable Ironman competitor, who, exhausted and worn down, still found it in him to cross that finish line before midnight.

The most resilient thing I've ever learned to do is this: keep finding meaning, passion, and joy—no matter what life brings.

Tragedy can strike anywhere and at any time, but you can never let it dim your light. This chapter is both a tribute to a life that ended too soon and a testament to the power of resilience. To keep riding—and loving—when both your legs and heart feel like breaking.

Chapter 8
Stand Your Ground

July 11, 1983: First "real" job, day two

Who would dare quit their first post-college full-time job on their second day of work? Turns out, I would. I had just the right combination of chutzpah and naivete to blow up my first opportunity and walk out the door—but I certainly didn't expect what came next.

It wasn't that I was in particularly high demand. Before graduating from Vassar College in May of 1983, I'd applied to several jobs, mostly at IBM, plus a management consulting role at a corporate accounting firm—none of which I landed. The son of an immigrant manicurist, I'd graduated with a degree in the relatively unknown field of cognitive science, plus some side gigs hustling hardware at Computerland.

My resume did not exactly scream "corporate leader."

Before heading on a summer trip to Greece with my first wife (then girlfriend), I applied to two more positions in the computer time-sharing industry, an early hot tech sector that—unbeknownst to me—was about to fall off a cliff. By mid-June, I was in Athens making long-distance calls from a taverna payphone near the Acropolis to decline one offer and accept another. I would start the first week in July.

Growing up, I knew exactly zero adults who worked at major corporations. Though I knew nothing about the corporate world, my mother's fierce determination and independence had taught me one thing: it was on me to control my destiny.

Whether I succeeded or failed, got promoted or fired, I wanted work based on a meritocracy whereas—in my college sales work—my talents and efforts counted. Given my lack of management experience and business connections, I figured it might prove difficult to gain access to, let alone effectively climb that corporate ladder.

Still, I had one family legacy to rely on: the survivor gene deeply encoded in my psyche. I was most comfortable depending on no one but myself. I knew how to trust my gut instincts and stand my ground. Sometimes to a fault, but more often to my advantage—even in the most unlikely of circumstances.

The week before my first day of work, still jet lagged from my Mediterranean getaway, I visited my new employer's Manhattan office at 350 5th Avenue, better known as the Empire State Building. I happily accepted when some of my new colleagues invited me to join them at a nearby bar. Maybe working full-time would be exciting after all!

What I learned at the bar shook me. Computer time-sharing, while revolutionary in the early days of high-cost, inefficient computing, now faced a serious threat. The rise of individual microprocessors in the early 1980s meant that computers no longer needed to share a central processor or memory, which had already caused a decline in our company's commercial accounts.

No amount of draft beer could counteract this sobering news: I was about to board a sinking ship. At least the company's Wall Street financial accounts remained strong—or so my companions told me. I spent the rest of the weekend with a pit in my stomach, trying to decipher what it all meant.

The following Monday, I showed up to my first day of work. My first assignment was to write software applications for commercial clients—the very department that, according to the scuttlebutt among my new work acquaintances, was going down first.

I returned home that evening to a blinking answering machine. I hit play to hear the voice of the hiring manager from the second company I'd interviewed with—demanding to know why I hadn't shown up for my "first day of work." Apparently, there'd been a misunderstanding in that transatlantic phone call from Greece; somehow, they thought I'd accepted their offer!

My eyes widened and my pulse quickened. *I may have made a huge mistake.*

So, what should an impressionable, know-nothing, 21-year-old Jersey kid do? The next morning, first thing, I walked right into my manager's office and announced my resignation.

As I saw it, the proper response should have been: "Don't let the door hit you on the way out!"

Instead, my boss ushered me into the vice president's office to talk me out of leaving. They asked why I wanted to go and what it would take for me to stay. I explained that it wasn't about money. I wanted to work with their Wall Street accounts.

Much to my surprise, they gave me what I wanted. I switched departments and stayed on for one year. After all, I'd just earned my first promotion—on day two of my first real job.

Just like that, I learned my first two valuable business lessons, the first being that you can't get what you don't ask for. More importantly, I affirmed that day that trusting my gut instinct—and standing my ground—would always lead me in the right direction.

No Regrets

Threatening to quit my inaugural job fresh out of college also allowed me to work directly with the company's vice president of sales, who became my first mentor and an invaluable early connection, helping me secure my next position and pivot to sales.

My second job was as an internal computer programmer at Burson-Marsteller, the world's largest public relations firm. Looking back, I realize this was an odd choice given my path of founding businesses, but I hadn't yet caught the entrepreneurial bug. Still smitten by the burgeoning computer industry, I set out to prove I had what it took to be a software engineer.

I liked writing software code. It's gratifying to leave the office knowing that you've actually *built* something. Even if all you did that day was write one line of code, that sure beats banging your head against the wall, making fifty cold calls in hopes of one sales prospect. At least, that's what I told myself.

But my second brief audition in the corporate technology world proved that I belonged elsewhere. It wasn't just office politics and the glacial pace of corporate decision-making. Before long, I had to admit it: I was a lousy software engineer. Writing good software code meant precisely following very specific rules and structures—my personal kryptonite. Like a roaring river, my creativity flowed free, along with my will to make my own rules.

When my first mentor got into mainframe human resources software, I left behind my misplaced dream of becoming a software engineer to work for him as a sales executive. By that point, I began to suspect I'd do better in a field where I could set my own pace and increase my earnings based on my skills and grit.

I must thank my first father-in-law—the late, beloved Henry–for helping me get on the sales track. I had just married his daughter, and at twenty-five, was already thinking about leaving a well-paying computer programming job for a risky software sales position. To me, this felt like an overwhelming decision fraught with risk.

Henry heard me out, then he told a story I would remember for the rest of my life. He explained that as a young man, he had ignored his early impulse to pursue an accounting degree. Instead, he listened to his father, who convinced him to work in the family's meat business. Although he did well financially, Henry always regretted not following his dream of building a career all his own.

His advice to me was simple and direct: "Do what you won't live to regret later."

I took the plunge, accepting the job selling mainframe human resource software. Not only did I never once regret that move, it also taught me about the high potential cost of ignoring your gut instincts. I've applied this advice to every major career choice I've made since.

A naturally competitive guy, sales suited me fine—especially the idea of keeping score. I soon rose to the top of my game. My first big commission yielded more than $50,000. Within the first two years, I rose to second highest-ranking salesperson and broke six figures. It felt great outselling my colleagues, measuring my progress, and above all, getting solid results from all my hard work.

From Sales to Startups

Just as I was hitting my stride—sure I'd found my rightful place in corporate America—I received a fateful call from an old Burson-Marsteller colleague I'd stayed in touch with, who, like my childhood friend, was also called Steve. He told me he had some big plans in mind, and he wanted to meet up with me to discuss an exciting opportunity.

"I'm starting my own company," Steve announced over drinks that evening. "And I want you to work for me."

I was instantly intrigued. Steve explained that he was looking to acquire ownership rights to a programming productivity tool from a company called Ross Systems. Using the jargon of the prehistoric 1980s, we called it a 4th generation language (4GL).

Steve had already become the premier consulting expert on this tool, and he wanted me to run his sales department. He offered me a solid job with a base salary, commissions, and a small piece of his new company.

"I'll join you on one condition," I told him. "That we work together—as co-founders and equal partners in the company."

We shook hands and, in the spring of 1988, flew to Palo Alto, California. In my first Silicon Valley trip, I helped negotiate a software intellectual property and ownership deal, and our company, Bizware, was born.

At age twenty-seven, I had become an entrepreneur, and there would be no turning back.

"In fact, I will"

Starting a software company with early Silicon Valley roots sounds far more exciting and glamorous than it was. The 4GL technology we purchased focused on accounting software, a business application I had yet to master. Plus, we had serious work to do before our little productivity tool could compete with industry leaders.

None of these obstacles mattered because I knew two things. First, the deal we struck came with a built-in customer base and a recurring revenue stream from annual maintenance fees. Second, with Steve's technical know-how and my sales and marketing talents, we made the perfect team.

I never had some grandiose vision of building Bizware into a large company and going public. I just wanted to make a good living, have fun, and preside over my destiny. That was enough for me to jump into the shark-infested waters of entrepreneurship.

But any success story includes twists and challenges. The day I almost fired myself from Bizware ranks among the most pivotal moments of my career.

It was roughly six months after we signed the deal, and business was good. We were steadily growing our revenue and customer base when the CEO and founder of Ross Systems decided to sell our parent company to a management buyout group. When they took Ross Systems into an initial public offering (IPO) in May 1991, Bizware's future fell into the hands of a new executive.

Suddenly, there was a new sheriff in town—one who seriously doubted the value of partnering with a small, Jersey software startup. I distinctly remember the new president suggesting we start looking for new jobs.

After a few frantic phone calls, we connected with this new CEO, who arranged to fly out to our offices, ostensibly to "negotiate new terms." He set one precondition for that meeting:

"I'll come out and talk as long as *that Cooper guy* stays out of the room," he said.

This new executive wanted to drive a wedge between co-founders, and I knew why.

Steve Wasserman and I have spent the majority of our careers together in the trenches. After meeting as colleagues, we'd go on to co-found and helm two companies. Perhaps more remarkably, our strong friendship survived it all and continues to this day. However, I noticed early on one significant business flaw in my friend—and made it my job to protect him from it.

Let's just say that when it came to negotiations, Steve was no shark. A naturally agreeable "yes man," he often deferred to me when it was time to say "no" to clients and business partners.

The new executive from Atlanta was emphatic about his preposterous demand. He wanted to intimidate Steve—and he succeeded. When Steve explained that I couldn't attend the meeting, I flatly refused to accept the terms.

"Oh, really? Seems to me that I *can* attend the meeting," I told my partner. "In fact, I will."

I needed to be in the room to show our new overlord we would not capitulate. Steve and I argued into the night until I finally put all my cards on the table. I told him I was willing to break up the partnership over this issue.

Steve finally consented. The day of the meeting, the two of us sat down with the recalcitrant executive. I challenged myself to play the part of the "strong, silent type," and by all measures, I succeeded. This meeting marked the first and last time I uttered so few words (most of them "no"). When the new Ross executive flew back to Atlanta, our deal remained fully intact, without changing a single letter of our contract.

The Real Prize

In the ten years of running Bizware, I learned through a combination of trial, error, and raw instinct how to launch and lead a company. Truthfully, it might be more accurate to say that I applied the innate skills that had already served me in direct sales: making tough decisions on the fly and standing my ground.

In 1998, Steve and I sold it back to the original software vendor, Ross Systems. They didn't need our technology or our customers, but the 21st Century clock was ticking, with

18 months to remediate their software applications from blowing up when the computer date turned over to 01012000. Ross Systems purchased Bizware because they needed warm bodies with tech talent to help them avoid Y2K complications.

The purchase price for Bizware comprised a neat sum of $2,000,000. Steve and I owned all shares and split the proceeds equally. I still remember the last conversation I had with the CEO of Ross Systems on the day we closed the deal.

"How does it feel to be a millionaire?" he asked.

"I don't know yet," I replied. "Ask me again when I have that much money in my hand."

He didn't bother, of course. In retrospect, perhaps my response sounded unappreciative. But I wanted him to know that I understood the legal fine print underpinning this deal.

As a publicly traded company, Ross Systems paid us out through restricted stock. However, the shares could only be sold in limited quantities over the course of one to two years. Due to market volatility, Ross' share price would yo-yo between the low $2 range and highs over $16.

While elated to close the deal and put some runs on the scoreboard, my excitement was tempered. Especially after taxes, even a one-time payout of the full million can be quickly lost to poor management. While this deal considerably improved my sense of security, it otherwise did not materially change my life.

Besides, I didn't start this business to get rich. I started it because I knew I could be successful and make a living. Far from sitting on my laurels, I instinctively knew this sale would lead to new challenges and even greater accomplishments.

After selling Bizware, I stayed at Ross System for one year. For once, I enjoyed working in a larger company and being part of corporate management. Still, I always needed to move forward. I worked at two other tech startups over the next three years, but all the while, there was something much bigger brewing.

I learned early on that if a company's purpose did not offer meaning beyond material gain, it would not fulfill me for long. As a young one-time entrepreneur, I determined never to live for my business, but rather to make my business live for me. That, to me, was the real prize.

Stand Your Ground

As a kid from the street with moxie and hustle, I could always make a buck. Running lunch orders to my mother's salon clients. Buying and selling t-shirts outside Shea Stadium. Even standing outside the local supermarket and—with no formal contract, permit, or permission—taking customers' grocery bags, shoving them in their cars, and holding out my hand with a smile to collect tips.

I can't say I wanted to become a tech entrepreneur when I first touched a computer keyboard in high school. Though enthralled with this promising new technology, I had no idea I would go on to found companies.

I also had no idea, as I dodged traffic pedaling through Manhattan streets, that I'd go on to compete in decades of bicycle races and complete ten Ironman triathlons.

I was only certain of one thing: I had the ambition and desire to find a career path and build the life that worked best for me. Looking back on my life spent following my gut and standing my ground, a few patterns emerge.

The first is the "Cooper Rule" of *just keep moving.* My gut instinct to always move forward has served me well in life, becoming my mantra of choice for my 10th and final Ironman race in Madison, Wisconsin. Moving backward or in the wrong direction is anathema to me, and stagnation is equally abhorrent.

If a job isn't challenging, I simply can't find it in me to focus. If I don't believe the company has a future or can't immediately see how it advances my career, I'm on to the next thing before the ink can even dry.

Finally, I need to control my livelihood and not let it control me. Throughout my career, this meant always maintaining a seat at the table. Even when I was too young to be anyone's boss—or when new leaders tried to block me out of vital decisions—I needed my ideas, opinions, and suggestions to be heard and valued.

There would still be two more startups in my future, but for now, I was still gaining traction in the business world. I knew my confidence and bravado could go a long way, but I still had trouble escaping my self-image as a yeshiva boy from Queens with few means and even less exposure to the business world.

No problem. I'd prove to myself—and everyone else—that I could rise to the occasion. My key takeaway from the first leg of my entrepreneurial journey—from navigating Bizware's early near-death experience to successfully selling the company—had to do with the power of conviction.

This means listening to your gut but also going further. Whether in business, endurance sports, or any area of life, you will reach a crucible where doubts and criticisms weaken your resolve, and you want to stand down.

Don't do it.

I'm not saying that my or anyone else's gut instinct is always right. But, in my experience, it's the best internal compass around. I've made a rule of staying the course until my gut—not some external naysayer (Atlanta executive or otherwise)—says otherwise.

Chapter 9
Be Consistent

February 14, 2023: Postoperative visit

"I'm sorry, but you do not understand my husband."

Ever the gracious diplomat, my wife, Beth, spoke these words at my two-week postoperative appointment to intercede on my behalf—as my nurse practitioner stood gaping at us, incredulous at what I'd just asked.

I guess she wasn't used to cancer patients requesting permission to go downhill skiing two weeks after a surgeon removed a deadly mass from their brains.

In my defense, it *was* February, the best time of year to ski in Colorado.

Jokes aside, this nurse practitioner saw dozens of patients a day, mostly people with relatively low activity levels and much slower recovery arcs than, say, a 10-time Ironman triathlon who's spent every spare moment of his adult life cycling, running, swimming, or sailing down snowy Denver slopes.

I'd expected the medical team to underestimate my post-op fitness level. Not to mention, my willpower and preternatural ability to know and respect my body's limitations...at least, most of the time. What I didn't expect was how much I'd have to temper my own recovery goals, both physically and, especially, mentally.

It had been almost five months since I'd raced Ironman Wisconsin on 9/11 through cold rain and heavy winds. Ultra-endurance sports are hard enough in perfect weather, but conditions that day added heavy layers of fatigue and strain to an already brutal feat. Many athletes didn't finish the race that day, and I could have easily been one of them. I didn't quit because I knew my sheer grit would carry me through.

Now, that inner grit was getting restless.

When I walked into the hospital for brain surgery, I had few expectations. When I walked out of the hospital two days later, my expectations instantly multiplied and rose sky-high.

I wanted to know when I could resume exercising, in what ways, and how often. When could I start working with various therapists to improve my cognitive and physical conditions? When would chemo and radiation treatments begin?

Despite my preaching to stay in the moment, for this part of the race with cancer, I couldn't help jumping ahead, imagining that I'd already crossed the finish line. While the successful surgery certainly counted as a victory to celebrate, I easily could—and did—indulge unreasonable expectations. That's why I'd resisted setting expectations for the surgery, so I could remain calm and focused.

With the operation over, those envelope-pushing, goal-setting habits bounced back with a new hunger.

While training, coaching, and conditioning all reliably improve triathlon results in healthy athletes, there are no guarantees in the race against cancer. Since I was no longer dealing with simple, fixed obstacles and objectives, I risked drowning in a sea of unmet expectations and false hope. For once, sheer force of will and brute effort would not get me where I wanted to go.

Fortunately, I had another IronCEO mindset principle to guide me through my expectation challenge: consistency.

Consistency builds mental muscle for doing hard things. As a triathlete, you need training consistency to cultivate strength and endurance. Rain or shine, whether you feel great or lousy, you need to get out there every day and do the work.

The same is true in business. As a leader, consistency means showing up; setting clear, realistic expectations; and staying the course to help your team execute. Especially in the professional realm, this also means setting emotions aside and keeping an even-keeled temper when something isn't working and you have to adjust course (something I admittedly haven't always been great about).

Now I had to take those hard-earned lessons and apply them to my biggest challenge yet. This meant honestly surveying my own limitations, and then setting recovery goals that challenged me without risking my health, safety, or demoralizing disappointment.

Finally, this meant staying the course, and showing up every day, whether that meant happily sweating away on a stationary bike, taking prescribed rest, or muddling through endless cognitive tests.

Return to the Pain Cave

The day I returned home after my initial surgery was beautiful: crisp, blue skies and highs pushing 50 degrees. A perfect day for a long walk in the park, following my surgeon's advice to "remain active and resume light physical activities."

First, I took a long and much-needed shower after three days without one. Then, my son, Evan, came over and drove us to Washington Park—known as "Wash Park" to us Denverites—for a brisk, two-mile walk along a paved loop.

It felt great to shake the cobwebs from my body and mind and breathe the fresh air of my favorite park, watching geese paddle around the lakes and greeting people walking or running along the path. Each moment of this New Year's walk with my son hit differently. This wasn't just the start of a new year, but of an entirely new chapter in my life, where every moment was a gift—not a given.

Now my idea of "remaining active" amounted to far more than simple strolls through the park. Still, it was just Day One. I reminded myself that, just as the body and mind need downtime to absorb and integrate the benefits of a hard workout, recovering from major surgery requires a bit of patience. While the precise balance of rest, easy exercise, and vigorous training differ from person to person, rest remained an essential part of my training process.

To me, "rest" looked like daily walks, starting with this two-mile New Year's hike and quickly growing to five to seven miles at a time. Sometimes, I walked alone or with a single friend or family member. Other times, an entourage of family or friends joined my walks in the park.

I knew the medical profession based its recommendations on the general patient's means. Since most people didn't train for triathlons in their spare time, "resume light physical activities" probably didn't much exceed one-mile walks and light housework. In my case, the doctors, nurses, and physical therapists would need to adjust to what worked for me.

If there was one activity dearest to my soul, it was cycling. I had biked over 100,000 miles since adulthood, and I didn't plan to stop anytime soon. The habit maintained an almost mystical hold on my life.

I didn't ask the medical staff for approval to resume biking. Beth was the only person of authority who understood both my need to get on the bike and my capabilities. She would support me.

I knew better than to ask for the moon. For now, riding a bicycle on Denver's streets, or even bike paths, remained out of the question. That request would come soon enough. Like any self-respecting bike fanatic, I already had the perfect solution for safe, comfortable riding during Colorado's winters: the Pain Cave—my elaborate garage cycling setup that would put any Peloton to shame.

Starting in my second week of recovery, Beth—my chief caregiver, therapist, and now-retired Ironman Sherpa—gave me the green light to return to the pain cave.

This may sound like an obsessive sixty-year-old man in denial about his cancer diagnosis and desperate to recapture some past glory. In truth, I wasn't concerned about getting back into "race shape." The goal was to keep my legs moving and my heart pumping hard enough to release much-needed endorphins. I knew the "high" I got from exercise would help keep my spirits high, regulate my mood, and maintain a good attitude—the benefits of which far outweighed physical conditioning. I was training my body and mind for a challenge much bigger than any triathlon race: my ongoing battle with incurable cancer.

A fixed bicycle going nowhere in my garage may not sound exciting, but it offered invaluable medicinal and mental benefits. There's a compelling, energizing rhythm to spinning the cranks on a bike. It's why spin classes caught fire among cyclists and non-cyclists alike. Whether you want to post out of the saddle and raise your heartbeat, or turn up the resistance and rock low revolutions, the effort is addictive. Put on your favorite music, movie, or bike race video, and next thing you know, you're sailing down the French Alps or roughing it through the Australian Outback—or just lost in your head and body.

For the avid cyclist, of course, nothing beats pedaling along a beautiful country road or flying down a mountain pass. I could sense it was only a matter of time before I would ride outside again. Neither a brain tumor nor a battalion of nurses could stop me.

Process > Progress

Walking? Indoor cycling? Check and check!

After a week of daily (if relatively restrained) blood-pumping aerobic movement, things were looking up. To gain a full quiver, I needed to add in yoga and light lap swims. I resumed my yoga practice early the second week but—at Beth's request—waited on approval from my medical team for swimming.

In my mind, a new goal was already taking shape. I dearly wanted to resume skiing, an activity I'd learned alongside the kids when they were still small, and one that formed a way of life among Coloradans.

The majesty of the mountains speaks to my soul. I experience awe, tranquility, and peace whether hiking up or skiing down. My raison d'être is the same whether skiing, long-distance cycling, running, or triathlons. It's less about the adrenaline rush and more about the serenity, calm, and internal stillness I experience when fully immersed in these activities. For me, cycling and skiing represent the best possible physical and mental therapy.

Before that two-week post-op visit with the nurse practitioner, I floated the idea past Beth. After eighteen years of marriage and twenty years of cohabitation, Beth had become my biggest advocate—but even still, she surprised me by supporting my bid to return to the slopes.

At the visit, we confirmed that thanks to Beth's home care, my surgical scar was healing nicely. I reported increased strength and energy with no ill effects. In short, I felt ready to add to my list of activities.

Given my spirited petition, sound reasoning, and backup from Beth, the nurse practitioner finally acquiesced to my demands to swim and ski. Perhaps it would be more accurate to say they accepted that I was going to do what I wanted either way. But they did lay down some ground rules. To avoid infection and ensure my surgery scars were properly healed, I (mostly) respected the nurse's decree to put off swimming until six weeks after the surgery—making it through week five before begging permission from Beth to get back in the pool a bit early.

In life, there are real limitations and self-imposed ones. It's important to know the difference. I was never going to run a five-minute mile or dunk a basketball, no matter how hard I trained. Instead, I needed to get realistic about where I could push limits and when I should practice acceptance or restraint.

Part of my IronCEO outlook involves what Stanford psychologist Carol S. Dweck calls a "growth versus fixed mindset." As she writes in her book, *Mindset: The New Psychology of Success*, "Brains and talent are just the starting point."

Individuals with a fixed mindset believe talent depends on natural ability. They tend to compare themselves to others, overemphasize personal limitations, and get easily discouraged. A growth mindset, on the other hand, is about achieving what's *possible* and stretching that threshold a bit further every single time.

Individuals with a growth mindset believe their abilities can be developed and limitations pushed through dedicated learning and hard work. They embrace challenges, see failures as opportunities for growth, and value effort as a path to mastery.

Above all, through *consistency of process*, they gain a lifetime of *progress*; a series of new "normals" that grow with them over time.

In terms of physical recovery, I'd have to accept that, this time, growth might not look like breaking past personal records in distance or speed. It wouldn't be measured in terms of miles or minutes, but rather in terms of mindset.

As much as I'd hoped the surgery would magically cure my neurological symptoms, my previous deficits in terms of dexterity, reflexes, and spatial awareness (among others) were still there.

Head Case

While my physical recovery was already exceeding all expectations, my cognitive rehab was quite another matter.

I'd felt perplexed when, at the two-week checkup, the hospital staff scheduled me to see a physical therapist and an occupational therapist. I didn't perceive my challenges to be physical or practical, but I decided to keep an open mind.

During my first PT visit, I learned from my therapist that, in addition to specializing in neurological disorders, he'd played division college hockey. This helped considerably to build trust and rapport, as I couldn't deny my bias towards medical providers with athletic backgrounds. I knew they'd better understand my needs and treat me accordingly.

I performed several simple tests for the physical therapist, including repeatedly sitting and standing for 30 seconds and doing a series of crossover steps known as "the grapevine." My scores exceeded the average for my age cohort, demonstrating a younger person's strength, stamina, and agility.

Though I'd never experienced balance issues or taken any falls (before or after surgery), I dutifully completed the prescribed exercises at home, mainly focused on increasing my perennial weaknesses: lower body flexibility and agility. While the drills did improve my agility, they could not fully correct the core physical or cognitive deficits related to coordinating the right side of my body.

I also knew that, while obsessive exercise had made me fit, my relatively inflexible, sixty-something-year-old body had always struggled with basic balance and mobility exercises. I once got pulled over by a police officer—sober as a judge—and failed to successfully walk a straight line.

Now my physical therapist asked me to do it again: putting one foot in front of the other, heel to toe. He even added a twist by instructing me to count backward from 100 by sevens or threes. I was barely able to stumble through backward threes. When I moved on to sevens, my pacing slowed to a crawl after "86."

I could not effectively multitask, and my brain was suddenly flummoxed by math. It felt nearly impossible to read aloud, let alone memorize, a 16-digit credit card number. Simple arithmetic, including basic addition and subtraction, tripped me up without a calculator. These cognitive deficits in short-term memory, math skills, and number confusion would require visits to speech and occupational therapists and cognitive assessments, including something called the Montreal Cognitive Assessment (MoCA).

To family, friends, and work peers, I appeared high-functioning. I could carry on an intelligent conversation on any topic. I could synthesize information as quickly and effectively as ever. I had no trouble finding words when speaking, and any slight hesitations in my speech were common at my age.

Still, my initial MoCA test scores came back below the norm, indicating mild cognitive impairment. In other words, despite appearances, I needed to proceed with at least some degree of humility and caution.

For someone with a voracious growth mindset, I wanted "consistency" to look like constant *improvement*. Now in at least some areas, it would have to mean showing up every day even when progress stalled.

This would take some getting used to.

"Disability" and Retirement

To thoroughly evaluate my cognitive abilities, I spent four tedious, exhausting hours at the hospital being interviewed and tested by a neuropsychologist. Their seven-page report contained many dry medical details describing my deficiencies, but two simple words tersely defined my main deficit: "executive function."

Executive function involves the ability to plan and execute goals, display self-control, follow multiple-step directions, and stay focused despite interruptions and distractions. I no longer demonstrated the competencies required for these tasks.

Without them, I could not return to work.

Before the surgery, I could only compose a long email, presentation, or proposal using speech-to-text, spell-check, and other productivity aids. Even then, my ability to focus, manage time, and organize my work (never my strong suits) held me back.

At first, I was determined to fix this, eager but sadly naive that I could get fast results. But after some time, I realized I had to accept and adapt to what was coming next.

Did I want to retire? Absolutely not. But like I said at the start of this book, I'd already had an inkling that new challenges lay ahead. To be honest, I didn't struggle as much as I thought I would with giving up work. I guess there's nothing like a terminal cancer diagnosis to help you re-evaluate life's priorities.

With a compelling enough reason, I can pretty easily shift my mentality of consistency from one goal—like endurance sports or business—to another. I had plenty to focus on with recovery, writing a book, and making the most of my time with family and friends.

Inner consistency means always committing to taking that next step, even when you aren't expecting it. While most people think of retirement in terms of hammocks and fishing trips, mine would involve physical, occupational, and speech therapy, in addition to upcoming radiation and chemotherapy.

But let's not get ahead of ourselves. The next step I had to take involved seeing an occupational therapist to help me improve my speech, language, cognition, and fine motor skills. I certainly had issues with all of the above, but because of my overall high level of cognitive function, I was a complex case—nonetheless, my demanding nature and high expectations made things any easier.

Goal Audit

I'd been reading about neuroplasticity even before my brain tumor diagnosis. I felt confident that, with the proper therapies, I could address my critical cognitive shortcomings. Unfortunately, I would soon learn that, despite my enthusiasm and diligence, there would be no quick fix.

My first speech therapy session began with paperwork and the usual checkup: heart rate, oxygen levels, blood pressure. I just wanted to get down to business. We started with simple card games designed to test my memory for numbers, patterns, and multitasking.

Once we got to more challenging drills, like memorizing lists of words, I realized my short-term memory had weakened considerably. The more I divided my attention among multiple tasks, the worse my recall of words, numbers, and sentences became. My weekly homework involved using science-based brain health apps to sharpen my cognitive skills.

These brain game apps were a mixed bag at best. Having come of age in the golden age of arcades, my interest in video games quickly waned. Steering simplistic computer graphics of different-colored trains of different colors along tracks felt somehow beneath me.

It was the math games that really did me in. I'd always taken for granted my natural affinity with numbers, from the early days of spreadsheets and college-level calculus to interpreting ledgers and developing financial models. Each time I drilled a math-based brain teaser math app, I faced a soul-crushing reminder of how far my skills had declined.

Nothing challenged a growth-mindset athlete like stagnation—let alone regression. One day, after an hour of struggle, my frustration unexpectedly boiled over. I slammed down my phone, buried my head in my hands, and broke down in tears—the first time I'd done so since my cancer diagnosis.

The final straw came as a fresh set of homework tasks designed to improve my right-hand motor skills. The therapist tasked me with cursive-writing letters and symbols multiple times on lined sheets of paper.

Fitness, whether mental or physical, is a use-it-or-lose-it proposition. My ability to legibly write in cursive was doomed the day I mastered speed-typing on a typewriter. The decline came slowly, decade after decade, but even before my brain tumor, I could barely scribble an intelligible handwritten note on a greeting card. Now, even that simple task had drifted far beyond my capabilities.

I found the alphabet exercise incredibly difficult and useless. It felt like recreating inscrutable hieroglyphics by hand. I desperately wanted improvement, but I needed help determining where my efforts would best be spent.

In terms of consistency, I had a choice to make. Should I dutifully stay the course, despite high levels of frustration and diminishing returns? Or should I adapt and let things go for the sake of my emotional well-being? Without more focused goals, it felt like we were chasing windmills—and I, for one, didn't have time for quixotic side quests.

It was time to do a serious audit: which impairments felt worth training, and which could I ignore? Desperate to figure this out, I did some thinking and, with the help of voice-to-text, prepared the following statement for my medical team:

"My physical limitations are small. I want to improve my balance and coordination well enough to be allowed to drive again, ride a bike outside, and continue to do the sports I enjoy, such as skiing. I have not experienced significant limitations when doing these activities. From a cognitive perspective, my speech is fine. While I have challenges with numbers, I am not overly concerned. I can use a calculator app or spreadsheet as needed.

"Main concern is my ability to type efficiently and form full, intelligible sentences. I may never be capable of returning to my current profession as a senior sales and business development executive because of my executive function deficiencies. That job relies heavily on typing, creativity, and business comprehension for creating presentations, proposals, and emails. However, I want to write my blogs and a book. Therefore, my main priority is regaining sufficient typing, spelling, word finding, and sentence structure skills to communicate effectively by the written word."

Those would serve as my marching orders. Luckily, my team appreciated the direction I'd given them and acknowledged that my expectations and needs differed from those of a typical patient.

I enjoyed working with my therapists, who were energetic, encouraging, and willing to customize my therapy. Nevertheless, my enthusiasm waned and I could not shake the doubt that I was wasting my most valuable commodity: time.

If there is one thing a stage 4 cancer diagnosis teaches you, it's to focus on the quality of life with the time you have left. Neither working full-time nor spending several hours a day copying cursive letters and doing math drills ranked high on my list.

So, at the end of March, barely five weeks into my therapy, I decided to pause all structured physical, speech, and occupational visits and focus on the best therapy I knew: exercise.

Back on the Road Again

Meanwhile, one specific practical goal survived this audit—and indeed, trumped all others: driving a car again. While my driving privileges had not been legally revoked, the surgeon and medical staff advised me to take a break after surgery.

Before I could safely resume driving, I needed to be evaluated by an occupational therapist and take the hospital's driving assessment. I could get back behind the wheel as soon as I passed the assessment and got my oncologist's consent.

Luckily, my OT had created driver assessment tools as a graduate project. With nothing more than paper plates, loose sheets of paper, and an iPhone to record reaction time, we created a kitchen-based driving simulation. She also assigned specific drills in an app called BrainHQ, which focused on reaction time with divided attention and processing periphery visual information.

When the date of my driving assessment arrived in March 2023, I aced the test, with my reaction times and other cognitive measures ranking similar to the average driver half my age.

With driving privileges restored, I regained independence and relief from family members and buddies hauling me everywhere. Still, I needed to ease back in. Beth insisted I start with short distances, avoid highways, stay off the cell phone, and never drive alone to the mountains.

Like most men, my hearing worked fine, but my *listening* skills could improve, especially when I didn't want to hear my wife's demands. This time, I knew not to push my luck. I didn't want to create additional worry for my wife. Brain cancer may never be a good thing, but life changes that cause you to become a better husband and human certainly are.

Peaks and Valleys

I'm aware that I began this chapter talking about consistency and ended it by admitting that I gave up on prescribed therapy. As I come upon the one-year anniversary of this decision, I sometimes wonder what I might have gained by continuing.

Upon reflection, my biggest downfall during therapy was always my own too-high expectations.

Anyone who thinks they can run an Ironman with little to no preparation is sadly mistaken. Coaches in the triathlon community accept the proven wisdom that it takes two years to train and prepare for your first Ironman distance triathlon. But I was far from accepting medical advice.

Still, there I was, taking shortcuts and thinking I knew better than trained professionals. Of course, they knew their jobs better than I did. But all of us were still in the dark about my life expectancy, and—in true IronCEO form, I've held strong.

Time is often the variable that overrides other factors. There's a benefit to thinking that every day is your last. When I finally threw up my hands to stop the various therapies, it was not a rash decision. I had taken stock of my life, carefully evaluated how I wanted to spend my remaining time and energy, and recalibrated my goals and expectations. Above all, I tempered my attachment to certain outcomes.

While this may have looked like inconsistency, I was trying to maintain a deeper equilibrium by getting honest about my goals and looking after my emotional health. As I said before, I haven't always been great about keeping an even temper when frustrated, and I couldn't afford to waste time getting upset while pursuing fruitless goals.

I knew my discipline, dedication, and hard work would restore my physical strength. However, my cognitive issues were largely out of my control. I had to step back into my lane and focus only on what I could control. That was the consistency that mattered most.

Luckily, I did not experience any further physical or cognitive decline since the surgery. I was a "two percenter," meaning: two percent slower, weaker, and less focused. I would take it and otherwise stay the course.

When consistency becomes a habit, it settles into your body and mind. Repetitions begin to assume their own inherent meaning beyond abstract future goals. This can help you persist even when you don't see or feel the desired results right away. It also frees up bandwidth so you engage in the actions differently, truly focused on *process* over outcomes. You no longer think about the work as a choice; you just show up and do it.

Until the time comes to recalibrate those goals and habits—and recommit. In a sense, adapting without fuss becomes its own form of consistency.

One thing has remained consistent anyway. I never did enjoy doing things halfway. My daily, monthly, and year-after-year exercise regimen for the triathlon served as proof. I also knew that trying to skip or rush through recovery ranked among the biggest mistakes athletes could make. When you condition yourself to regularly push beyond failure, it's easy to lose sight of recovery as a training discipline—and much harder to stay consistent and measured.

So, I adapted and recommitted to the recovery journey in my own way. Cyclists know more than anyone that every hill or mountain has both a peak and a valley—and that you can't define yourself by either your highest peak or your lowest valley. Instead, you must accept your ups and downs as nothing more than transitions to the next phase of the journey.

Chapter 10
How to Succeed—and Fail

April, 1993: Enter Bruce

Far from a neat and orderly "corporate ladder," a more apt metaphor for the entrepreneurial career path would be rafting down a Rocky Mountain-fed river. You have a good idea of where you're heading—until tributaries split. Suddenly, you shift from serene sailing into high alert: navigating rocks, waves, eddies, and whirlpools. This requires a combination of receptivity and decisiveness: the ability to both go with the flow and make quick choices under pressure. The chosen path becomes the way, even if you don't quite know what's coming next.

This is how I've lived my professional life, instinctively open to new connections, experiences, and opportunities. First, my modus operandi took me to Steve, and our software and consulting company, Bizware. Next, it brought us into a meeting with a gentleman named Marvin, who described an even bigger vision: innovating financial services with a social impact bent.

It was 1992, and Steve and I had just hired a new Bizware employee, Bruce, to work in business development. One day, Bruce tipped me off about an interesting new business venture. His former colleague, Marvin, was raising money for a startup called In-Person Payments (IPP). I had Bruce set up the first meeting.

When Marvin walked into my office a week later, we both smirked as I recognized his wry, winning grin and stout build. Turns out, we'd been direct competitors back when I sold mainframe HR software. Because I was regularly winning deals against his sales team, Marvin had his recruiter entice me to take a job with a different HR software company—one that was not his direct competitor. The universe truly is a small place.

The pitch Marvin gave us that day would mark a turning point in my career. It was the first time I'd heard the term "unbanked." Before that, I had never sent a money order or cashed a check outside of a bank, and I knew nothing about automated clearing house (ACH) electronic networks or money transmission licenses. Still, Marvin told a compelling story: more than 30 percent of American adults lived paycheck-to-paycheck in the early 1990s, using alternative financial service providers instead of banks and paying their utility bills either in-person or through mail-in money orders.

Marvin's fledgling start-up would offer these customers cheaper bill-pay services at more convenient times and locations. Instead of everyone lining up at the utility office on the first of the month or mailing in money orders, customers could go to a check cashing kiosk or other local agent locations for bill pay. Because this arrangement also benefited utility companies, they were willing to absorb more of the processing fees, reducing customers' financial burden.

The company had a definable and expansive niche, and Marvin's predecessor company had already proved the use case and customer need. For IPP to launch, they needed more technology plus a few million dollars. In 1993, the investment community was not too keen on startups offering both economic return and social value for unbanked populations. It was a tough sell then and remains so today.

Neither Steve nor I had the means to make a significant investment, but Bizware had plenty of programming resources and processing capacity on our minicomputer. By the end of the meeting, I wanted in.

Our subsequent experience with IPP, followed by my third and final—this time, solo—venture would teach me a lot about the nature of success. I learned (often the hard way) about the value of listening to criticism and understanding my core, driving motivations. While such realizations come as a shock to a young entrepreneur who thinks he's got it all figured out, my most valuable lessons had more to do with the nature and value of failure—something that, up until that point, I'd refused to factor into my plans.

Ups and Downs

After that initial meeting, we made Marvin an offer he did not immediately accept, but I knew he couldn't refuse.

Bizware would build and run the software applications to process customers' bill payments, which intellectual property would eventually transfer to Marvin. In return, he would give us a significant share of IPP's equity.

After some back-and-forth, we signed the business agreement and started building the software. Marvin meanwhile shared his industry know-how and recruited our initial network of bill consolidators and financial services agents. While our partner worked IPP full-time, Steve and I could help build this company on the side, while maintaining Bizware operations.

Within our business model, agents at corner drug stores and other money services locations could buy or lease an IBM PC to run our software, along with a Hayes 1200 baud modem to transmit payments each evening to our central computer. Before the widespread use of the internet, this was state of the art.

Three months later, IPP officially launched when our first agent location in Paterson, New Jersey, transmitted its first daily batch of bill payments. I remember the exact moment we went live in the spring of 1993. We stood in our Bizware office and cheered as the receiving modem erupted into a series of beeps, whistles, and clicks before accepting the first analog data transfer. These transfers would occur each evening after Bizware's usual operating hours to avoid noisy disruptions from the dial-up modem—unforgettable sounds that stir nostalgia among those who know.

IPP was not an overnight success. Without outside capital initially, we had to rely on sweat equity to build the software and grow our agent base and payment volume. At its height, IPP processed more than one million monthly bill payments through an agent network in over 30 States. It took us ten years to get there.

As co-founder and investor—and later, board member and strategic advisor—I had the catbird seat to observe IPP's ups and downs. During the first decade, my role evolved from software designer into business development, setting up partnerships beyond direct points of sale with companies that could add our tech to their financial products.

In 2003, ten years after Marvin visited my Bizware office for the first time, I came on board as a full-time IPP to direct business development. Even at IPP, which had about 50 employees at the time, I had to create the right job. Plus, my bona fide record proved I could sell almost any technology solution. Still, I wanted to do something other than sell things. I wanted to focus on what I enjoyed: building products, organizations, and businesses.

A sales organization requires pricing, collateral material, an understanding of the competition, and a prospect list. If one or more variables involving the company's product, market, or target customer are undefined, you need someone skilled in multidisciplinary business development.

Within eighteen months of joining IPP full-time to run business development, over 50 percent of our new locations and agent payment volume came from indirect channels I had sourced. These included stand-alone kiosks, point-of-sale stores offering financial products like long-distance prepaid phone cards and wireless top-ups, and alternative financial service providers integrating our bill pay tech into their check cashing platforms.

For the next few years, Steven remained a part-time founding partner while Marvin and I directed the ship toward ever-expanding horizons. Though we enjoyed the thrill of business growth, we also maintained a sense of balance rarely enjoyed by today's fast and furious fintech startups. Marvin didn't believe in sacrificing every second of his life to work. Though we worked hard to maintain business growth, Marvin wasn't one to skip meals or work through the night. Every Thursday he enjoyed a leisurely lunch of kielbasa and pierogies at a local Polish deli, often bringing me and others along.

Overall, those were heady times for IPP and me personally. After we finished raising our second venture capital (VC) round, it seemed to us the sky was the limit.

Then it all came crashing down.

Growing Pains

One day in 2007, while Marvin was out to lunch, a team of investigators from the Essex County Special crimes unit burst into our New Jersey headquarters and confiscated

Marvin's computer. Marvin was later arrested but never tried or convicted on any criminal charges.

To make a long story short, IPP wasn't growing fast enough for VC investors, prompting concern and suspicion. We could have kept expanding at our sustainable, steady rate, but once a company takes on VC money, the stakes and expectations abruptly change. Once you're beholden to outside investors, it's time to seriously ramp up strategic reinvestments into company growth to surge profits far beyond what Marvin's more moderate tendencies could deliver.

Though he was ultimately cleared of any wrongdoing, this incident so deeply shook our investors and board members that they voted Marvin out of the company he'd founded. He reluctantly resigned after accepting a cash buyout on all his company shares.

With a new CEO coming in to shake up the team, I knew the writing was on the wall. I could have stayed on but at the expense of the role I'd created for myself. The new chief wanted to bring in his own business development leader. In the end, I negotiated the same buyout deal, along with a one-year employment contract.

While IPP remains my greatest entrepreneurial achievement, it was far from the success it could have been. The new owners later sold IPP to the kiosk company, Tio Networks, for $40 million. After PayPal acquired Tio, they worried that the walking bill payment operation we had pioneered might open the company to potential security breaches. Rather than investing in confirming the issue and innovating solutions, they simply dropped the services.

Looking back, it's clear now that Marvin should have financed our company through a bank or other lender, rather than tapping VC funding. Venture capitalists tend to expect one of two outcomes. The first is that the company succeeds spectacularly and—either through an initial public offering

(IPO) or company sale—the VC gets a big win and the limited partners get their expected return on capital. The second (far more likely) outcome involves anything from outright failure to a longer-term grind of mid-range success—it's all the same to a VC. Close to 90 percent of startups will eventually fail. Venture capitalists make their money hunting the unicorns from the first group. You're as good as dead once they believe you belong to the latter cohort.

Marvin wanted VC investments to strengthen our balance sheet and meet the requirements and covenants IPP needed for our many state money transmission licenses and surety bonds. While this represented a valid use of investment proceeds, and even though IPP pulled a profit, VC investors demanded greater returns on capital. Marvin wanted to run IPP as a lifestyle business, meaning we could grow conservatively and organically, making decent money over the long term.

This experience with IPP felt bittersweet because, with a different funding approach, we easily could have done what Marvin hoped for. But when you take other people's money—specifically from venture capital or private equity firms, you need to strategically and obsessively reinvest to keep scaling.

Marvin was a good CEO and leader. Calm and steady under pressure, he could captain the ship around any oncoming obstacle. But once the sky cleared and the water calmed, Marvin would settle in, content to sail on rather than chart new courses into the unknown.

Meanwhile, I inherited the survivor's restless need for forward momentum. Finding new ways to accelerate growth has always been part of my DNA. With new lessons learned, I felt ready to forge ahead into uncharted waters.

Solo Venture

A savvy investor will tell you that good ideas are a dime a dozen; the real money and value come through the execution. I wanted to prove I could start and build a company independently, without a partner, and execute. So, in 2013, I launched Rezzcard. This would serve as the culmination of everything I had learned in the past twenty years.

Like IPP, Rezzcard was a company with a social impact mission serving the underbanked and unbanked US population. While a growing startup boom focused on the burning need for comprehensive financial products for this massive population, my objective with Rezzcard only tackled one problem: making monthly rent payments more convenient and less expensive for the financially underserved.

Many landlords refused checks from lower-income tenants, forcing them to pay cash in person or purchase money orders to mail in or hand-deliver. The Rezzcard platform allowed these individuals to pay their rent seven days a week from more convenient locations, and it would typically be posted to their accounts within one business day. For the price of a money order, customers could make all their bill payments, including rent, using our previous network of IPP retailers. This greatly reduced the lines outside rental offices on the first of each month while accelerating the speed of transactions.

Rezzcard enjoyed some early traction, especially after I signed the public housing authority in Newark, New Jersey—one of the largest in the country—along with several leading affordable housing property managers in New York City. Although this first phase of growth energized me, I didn't swing for the fences boldly enough. Just as quickly as transaction volume improved, growth began to plateau.

Before long, it became clear I wouldn't succeed in growing Rezzcard past our initial wave of early adopters to further scale the company's trajectory. Customers began switching to electronic credit card payments using online platforms, and in 2017, I sold the company to MocaFi, a financial services startup focused on the American underbanked. While this was a fire sale and stock-only deal, I was proud that I found a good buyer that didn't leave my investors holding the bag. Meanwhile, my previous entrepreneurial gains meant I could personally absorb the remaining losses.

Nevertheless, after thirty years in the tech industry and two successful startups, I consider Rezzcard my first failure. MocaFi couldn't make it work either and eventually shut down the rent payment service.

Learning from Losses

While this final leg of my entrepreneurial journey was the shortest and least successful, it taught me the most valuable lessons of all.

First, I learned the true value of finding a solid business partner. Being a solo entrepreneur is often a lonely journey. To navigate all the challenges of running and growing a business—from building capital to developing a board and stellar executive team—you need someone you can trust to always have your back. If you find the right fit, your partner will bring complementary talents to fill in the gaps left by your weaknesses. After starting two successful companies with partners, I decided to go solo with Rezzcard. At the time, I knew the odds of success improved with a co-founder, so why did I make this move?

The reason is as stupid as it is revealing of my psyche. With the first two ventures, I'd executed someone else's idea. This time, I felt I had something to prove by starting my third company alone.

Many entrepreneurs can relate to my second egregious mistake: I had convinced myself that I knew the problem I was solving better than anyone else, and therefore offered the best solution.

This false narrative left me resistant to critical feedback and new information that didn't already confirm my biases. I focused my attention primarily on the rent-paying residents, rather than the *real* customers: the property managers and housing authorities. To them, Rezzcard only solved part of their problem. Meanwhile, competitors in the growing fintech industry increasingly marketed electronic rent-pay solutions to affordable housing tenants. I tried to add these capabilities, but that pivot proved too little too late.

People like to say that Steve Jobs used some kind of "reality distortion" field to bend reality to fit his desired purposes, convincing others to back his ideas no matter how improbable they seemed. Obviously, though, charisma and smarts only went so far.

Every successful entrepreneur needs to perfect two seemingly opposed skill sets. First, you need blinders to ignore all the naysayers and contrarians who initially oppose your innovative business idea. However, the opposite principle also stands: while you must believe in yourself and your basic business idea beyond reproach, a good entrepreneur must also—constantly—accept critical feedback and new information to determine if and when to change course.

Embedded within this paradox is the greatest—and simplest—entrepreneurial lesson: Failure is an option.

I now know that it's okay to fail, but I grew up thinking I couldn't fail. This latter conviction was the most influential belief throughout most of my entrepreneurial career.

I did not hold this belief because I thought everything I touched would turn to gold. Instead, I was simply being pragmatic. As the son of a poor immigrant, I grew up watching my mother raise me alone. A consummate survivor, Susan Cooper knew that she could not afford to fail, so she acted accordingly, working long hours and throwing everything she had into earning by whatever means she could.

Not only did I inherit this survivor mindset, I'd also launched my career without a safety net. I had precious few resources to rely on, so I refused to acknowledge the many (very real) risks involved. It's not that I feared failure exactly; I simply could not entertain it. To me, failure was a luxury for those who could afford a backup plan.

Considering what a liability this mindset proved to be, my entrepreneurial career went unexpectedly well. It took time to realize that truly avoiding failure demanded the acceptance of failure as a potential outcome first. Only then could you fully assess and appreciate the risks involved, and develop plans and contingencies to mitigate those risks. This also helped founders listen to feedback, discern when the ship strays off course, and both accept and adapt to problems before they threaten to sink their entire operation.

Success requires a strong vision, but vision alone won't get you there. Avoiding failure demands humility and an understanding of your weaknesses. If I'd been able to more critically examine my assumptions and shortcomings, I likely would have brought in a trusted partner, better listened to customers, and abandoned the negative belief that I had something to prove.

I can now call myself a success without question. However, like beauty, success lies in the eye of the beholder. By any objective standard, I've filled my career with accomplishments. I provided for my family, lived comfortably, and achieved significant career milestones. However, I've never been one to measure by the numbers, whether the metric relates to companies started or income earned.

Numeric goals can help motivate action, but for me, they're no more meaningful than the box of race medals I have stashed away in a closet somewhere. The thrill of hitting your sales numbers or finishing an Ironman wears off quickly. I instead measure accomplishments by the internally driven state of joy, happiness, and satisfaction derived from doing something *meaningful.*

Lately, the concept of "finding your why," has gotten a lot of buzz—and for good reason. Without a powerful core motivator, you'll lack the commitment and passion to keep up the grind and "hit the numbers."

Guy Kawasaki, the early Apple employee turned Silicon Valley venture capitalist and author, famously said, "Great companies start because the founders want to change the world...not make a fast buck."

My advice to aspiring founders begins with this question: Why are you willing to risk everything, work harder than you ever imagined, and—at least initially—forgo a steady paycheck? I happen to agree with Guy Kawasaki; if you're not looking to change the world, don't even bother.

My entrepreneurial journey focused on bringing value, helping others fulfill their vision, and making a difference—while doing it my way. In these respects, I can call myself a success.

I also, admittedly, strayed off course. Namely, I started Rezzcard for all the wrong reasons. In part because I'd convinced myself I wouldn't fail if I couldn't, I decided to go it alone—without a partner. Instead, I wanted to prove myself, to show everybody: *look at what I can do by myself.*

In the end, we must all define for ourselves what qualifies as "success"—in a way that accounts for inevitable failures and lessons from them. When it comes to starting a business, some shoot for the stars. Others, like Marvin, would be happier with a "lifestyle business" they slowly grew and never sold. While I remained somewhere between these two extremes, in the end, my commitment to family and endurance sports tempered my entrepreneurial mania.

I keep coming back to this word, *meaning*. According to Guy Kawasaki, you need a strongly rooted sense of meaning to endure what it takes to become a successful entrepreneur. Even when it comes to surviving atrocities like the Holocaust, the author Viktor Frankl's words say it all: "The greatest task for any person is to find meaning in his or her life."

Pursuing meaning helped me both achieve entrepreneurial success and—ultimately—accept and learn from my failures.

Later, as the reality of brain cancer brought an abrupt end to my career and reduced my athletic pursuits, I would have to slow down, revise and abandon some goals, and uncover new layers to life's meaning.

THIRD LEG:
Connections, Compassion, and a New Kind of Endurance

Chapter 11
You Are an IRONMAN

June 29, 2014: My first Ironman

To the uninitiated, Ironman requires a serious sanity check. It starts with a 2.4-mile outdoor swim, followed by a 112-mile bicycle ride, and then it all wraps up with a full marathon run of 26.22 miles. Participants typically begin the race around 7 a.m. and have about sixteen hours to reach the finish line by midnight—the cut-off distinguishing a successful race from a technical "did not finish" or DNF.

Intimidating doesn't begin to describe it. Dedicated, passionate triathletes understand that Ironman is less a sport than a lifestyle—seven days a week, 52 weeks a year of regimented nutrition, rest, and training, including scheduling, traveling to, competing in, and recovering from shorter triathlons and other "practice" races. It's all-encompassing for both participants and the families that accommodate and support these obsessions.

I was not "in the know" when I signed up for my first Ironman distance race in mid-2013, almost a year before the

June 2014 event in Atlantic City, New Jersey. I had recently turned fifty-one, and at the time, racing an Ironman was just another goal I wanted to do at least once before checking it off the list.

I'd done shorter triathlons in my late twenties and early thirties but stopped due to the demands of raising young kids. I remember watching the iconic Ironman Championship races, held annually in Kona, Hawaii, on television. Those men and women were *real* athletes: fit, fast, and determined to finish the most grueling one-day sports event on the planet.

That wasn't me. I was just a middle-aged guy out for endorphins and a little exercise. In my mid-forties, when the kids became teenagers, I got back into triathlons, building up to the shorter Olympic (.93-mile swim, 24.8-mile bike, 6.2-mile run), and half-Ironman-distance events (1.2-mile swim, 56-mile bike, 21.2-mile run).

Finishing a Half Ironman took most people in my class of competitors five to six hours, in addition to serious training and time commitment. But competing in a full Ironman demanded a quantum leap in fitness and dedication. Unless you already ran marathons or regularly biked over 100 miles a week, it was hard for most people to even fathom—but in the back of my mind, I always wondered if I had what it took to go the full distance of 140.6 total miles.

Having now completed ten Ironman races in as many years, I can tell you that getting to the start line of an Ironman triathlon is much more daunting than finishing it. If you have the courage to show up on race day, the rest is easy.

If you don't believe me, just show up as a spectator to watch the last few hours of any Ironman race. The real drama begins around 10 or 11 p.m., long after the professionals and elite athletes have crossed the finish line and gone home—leaving the rest of us age groupers and competitors of all shapes, sizes, and conditions, including those with average to overweight physiques and even physical disabilities or prostheses.

Late into the evening, with the midnight time cut-off looming large, you see nothing but smiles, tears, and arms raised in victory.

What separates such "ordinary" Ironman from anyone else is only our incredible will and determination. Our only desire is to complete the race before the race clock strikes midnight, a desire that overcomes incredible fatigue, pain, and doubt.

This is the true measure of endurance. One that's available to anyone who can believe themselves capable of crossing that finish line, and—most importantly—who has the courage to start what they'll finish.

Start Small & Build Habits

Merriam-Webster defines *endurance* as "the ability to exert oneself and remain active for a long period, as well as withstand, recover from trauma, wounds or fatigue." Someone with exceptional endurance may appear exceedingly physically or mentally strong—but eventually, every single one of us wears down to a state of unimaginable fatigue. The trick is to keep going anyway.

I learned early in life while observing my teammates that I had to look after myself, challenge limitations, and work hard for everything I achieved.

As a kid in team sports, it's natural to compare yourself to others. You motivate yourself through competition, numeric goals, and rankings. But many people lose the drive to push themselves as they get older, and team sports dissolve into office hours and parenting responsibilities. At this point, endurance must become a conscious habit that you build every time you overcome something you never thought you could.

It all begins with small habits.

Starting (or breaking) any habit takes practice and dedication. You only build physical and mental muscle through routine and mundane repetition. After a while, you no longer have to think about it; you just do it.

Because it all starts with daily habits, anyone can train endurance, whether that means physical racing, developing a talent, or putting in the extra mile at work. Whether you want to cultivate a new habit like daily runs, meditation, chanting affirmations, or even just getting an earlier start to your day, repetition helps internalize the pattern, so it becomes second nature.

Numerous mobile apps have been designed to take aspiring athletes from couch potatoes to 5K. They all seem to follow a basic principle: start slow and stay consistent. Maybe at first, you just run five minutes and walk one, then repeat that a few times a week, gradually increasing the frequency and duration before building in some gentle cross-training.

Likewise, I began with easier distances, starting with sprint triathlons of about sixteen total miles and working up to Olympic and half-Ironman-distance events, sometimes in the company of family members, like my daughter, Jess. She proved to be my most enduring Ironman partner—and one who would quickly prove capable of leaving her old man in the dust. My son also did a couple of half-Ironmans, mainly to humor me. (A consummate all-or-nothing guy, Evan instinctively knew the full Ironman experience could swallow up his life, including his dedicated marathon running habit that sometimes delved into ultramarathon distances.)

You meet all kinds of people on Ironman courses. From all walks of life, backgrounds, and fitness levels. It's not always easy, at first glance, to tell who's going to finish. As someone who enjoys helping and hyping up others, I could always be seen cheering my fellow racers along the way.

Encouragement helps, but true endurance comes from within.

I remember at one half-marathon training event, I encountered a woman who had completely psyched herself out. She couldn't stop thinking about how many miles we had left to go. I reminded her to stay in the moment. Given that she was a yoga teacher, I pointed out that she could apply the same meditative approach to focus only on the next step. She had gotten too flustered, and in the end, I couldn't save her from her mental spiral—so I just sped up to avoid further draining myself.

Most of the time, though—and always when it came to Jess—I found that fellow competitors inspired me as much as I inspired them. A special camaraderie arose out of this community of people who all showed up for themselves, no matter the odds. Who began with small, everyday habits, then somehow went on to achieve the seemingly impossible.

Going the Distance

My first full-distance race was held in Atlantic City, New Jersey, in June 2014, just a 2.5-hour drive from my house in North Jersey. The convenient location and pancake-flat terrain of the city's Triathlon Park in Bader Field made this a perfect opportunity to test my mettle.

It was finally time to throw my hat in the Ironman ring—*Ironman distance*, anyway. ("Ironman" is a trademarked brand owned by The Ironman Group, and no other race organizer or publication—including this book—can call a non-official race of these distances "Ironman.")

The first thing you learn about a full-distance, 140.6-mile, triathlon race is that there are no easy courses. It was intensely hot that day, with a poorly laid-out swim course and brutal ocean headwinds slowing down even the fastest cycler.

Normally, the swimming course is in a lake or river, with a rectangle or triangle of buoys laying out the course. The parks' ocean bay was anything but calm or easy, with currents, whirlpools, multiple turns, and areas so shallow or thick with reeds that even the strongest swimmers registered poor swim splits.

In addition to the seventeen-hour overall requirement to finish the race, you must finish each leg by a set time or risk disqualification: two hours and twenty minutes to finish the swim, then ten to ten and a half hours from the initial dive into the water to the start of the run.

Foolishly, I set specific numeric goals for my first full-distance triathlon, estimating in advance how long each leg of the race would take me. I was a strong cyclist, an average runner, and a relatively slow swimmer. So, my math equation for finishing the Ironman was simple: if I could survive the swim without drowning or missing the cut-off, I would have a "comfortable" amount of time: six to seven hours on the bike and five to six hours for the run before the clock struck midnight.

All expectations were blown out of the water after that first—long and deflating—swim. When I saw the final buoy and race banner marking the end of the first leg, I swam as hard as I could, leaving the water with mere minutes to spare before I would have had to register a DNF. My wife was relieved I wasn't on a rescue boat clinging for my life. My kids were just happy they didn't have to spend the rest of the day with a soggy, pissed-off dad.

Thrilled that I wasn't disqualified, simply surviving that harsh swim provided a boost of confidence. If I could swim for more than two hours in those conditions and still feel strong, I could tackle anything else the day would bring.

That marked my first valuable lesson for racing an Ironman: while goals are admirable, the true secret to finishing lay in managing expectations and keeping your head in the moment—not thinking about the final result. I learned not to let my thoughts drift to what was coming down the pike. My focus had to stay in the right here, right now. If I could do that, I soon learned, the rest would take care of itself.

All told, I managed to finish that first race in a respectable time of thirteen hours and thirty-seven minutes. I'll never forget the first time my name got announced over the finish line loudspeaker, declaring me among the Ironman ranks. Though exhausted and hungry, I floated on cloud nine, oblivious to the state of my body. I'd wanted to prove I had what it took to finish this race, and I was happy to check one more item off my bucket list.

A few days later, my aches dissipated, my joints and muscles began moving normally, and the exhaustion began to leave my body. What I didn't expect was the enduring glow left behind. A soul fire sparked within me after I achieved something as special as a 140.6-mile distance that doubled any racing feat I'd previously achieved.

Without intending to, I had begun a decade-long journey of endurance, where a combination of perseverance and passion could take me to places I'd never been. I was ready to make Ironman a part of me.

For the Long Haul

That didn't mean that I, a man starting Ironman in his fifties, would greatly improve from race to race. After starting with numeric goals—and quickly becoming humbled by reality—my second race wasn't substantially faster. I didn't care. I was in this for the long haul, to see just how far I could take it, regardless of the numbers.

In 2014, I did two Ironman races. That year, I felt so good after completing the first summer event in Atlantic City, that I signed up for the October North Carolina Ironman called "Beach2Battleship."

The second race marked the first full Ironman I ran alongside Jess. Because I knew she'd considerably outpace me, we made plans to meet up at a stopping point where you can rest and replenish nutrients, about halfway through the course. Then we'd tackle the rest of the bike ride and the run together.

I completed that swim in less time than usual, largely because the course featured an easy one-way channel with water currents flowing in our favor. (I later joked that even a bag of potato chips could have done that leg in an hour.) Next, I enjoyed a relatively easy bike course and a helpful wind at our backs.

Still, as soon as I arrived at our rendezvous, I learned Jess had already been waiting nearly ten minutes. I knew she'd be faster—but I hadn't expected that much!

"Go ahead without me," I said, stopping to catch my breath and assured her I'd catch up on the bike.

It took me a good fifteen minutes of hustle to do so, and only because she slowed down. From there, we finished the second leg before racing the marathon run side-by-side. I knew Jess was the stronger runner, but she stuck with me the whole way. Reveling in the joy of sharing this experience with my daughter—and determined not to let her down—I pushed myself harder than I ever had before.

That was my daughter's first Ironman event, and despite her dad slowing her down, we both finished in respectable times. In fact, this race marked my "career best" time at eleven and a half hours! (I typically remained in the thirteen to fifteen-hour range.)

Every time my kids and I have raced, together or not, and regardless of our finish times, I remain most proud of them—and myself—for just showing up at those start lines.

In the end, adjusting expectations is all part of the sport. When I had climbed out of the water after the first leg of my first Ironman and realized I'd escaped disqualification by minutes, I learned to humble myself, adapt, and push forward.

One-man Victory, 2020

Every one of my ten Ironman races was memorable for their own reasons. Crossing the Ironman finish line for the very first time in Atlantic City—with Beth and the kids there to see it—would always stand out. For my 2016 race in Mont Tremblant, Quebec, the organizers put on a pre-race banquet of live performers that made us racers feel like real celebrities. Finally, the courses in both Lake Placid and Madison (despite the terrible weather during the latter) were both stunning locations with great vibes.

But one race stood out among the others—and it wasn't even an official Ironman.

The year was 2020, and everything—including the Ironman Group—was on lockdown. Still, I was determined to keep my one-race-a-year streak alive. So, with some help, I created my very own Ironman distance race in Colorado, "in my backyard."

I met my family—Jess and my son-in-law, Mike—and some dear friends at the reservoir in Chatfield State Park in Littleton at 6 a.m. on September 12, 2020. We'd already scoped out the swim route for the first leg and set up tables in the park for my fans to cheer me on. The second leg began at the Chatfield reservoir, then took me south toward Palmer Lake before looping back to ride along the Platte River bike path to Wash Park in Denver, where I'd run the third leg.

As I said in an IronCEO video I made at the time, doing a triathlon of this magnitude is off the crazy charts for most people. Doing it without thousands of fellow athletes and cheering supporters, with no prizes, no Mike Riley, no hoopla—that's just batshit.

Arriving at the reservoir and putting on my wetsuit, I felt a curious mix of adrenaline-infused excitement and introspective calm. In such an isolating and strange year as 2020, getting to still do what I loved most among the people I loved most made me realize I was not alone. (In fact, in addition to my loved ones, I randomly found two other people racing their own solo Ironman-distance triathlons at Chatfield that very morning!)

My Ironman daughter served as my Ironman Sherpa. With some help from my New Jersey buddy, Craig, she coordinated supplies, checkpoints, and transitions for the race. She also took turns with Mike, Craig, and a few trusted friends pulling me on the bike (i.e., riding in front of me) and pacing me along like a bat outta hell for 112 miles—at a personal record-setting pace. This technically violated Ironman race rules against drafting (and likely shaved an hour off my biking time), but Triathlon USA officials can cancel me if they want. *My race, my rules.*

Finally, someone joined me on every running lap around Wash Park for that final leg—including my all-time favorite running companion, Beth, who kept pace almost stride by stride with me for about ten miles of that marathon. I loved seeing the trademark IronCEO smile on her face. For those miles she ran with me, it felt like my feet never even touched the ground.

This was hands-down the most fun I ever had doing a race. While I may not have had "the Voice of Ironman," Mike Reilly to announce my finish, I did get to experience breaking through the finish line ribbon for the first time ever. Sure, it was a makeshift ribbon of toilet paper held up by my kids, but that just added to the fun.

Most of all, I got to share this intense triathlon experience with my biggest fans in a participatory way. I barely even looked at the clock for time splits or mileage. I just swam, biked, and ran like I was hanging out all day with my besties. (Which, of course, I was.)

This one-man victory ranks as my all-time favorite Ironman distance race. I may not have *officially* earned the title that time, but I truly felt like an Ironman that day. Mainly because I realized what a gift it was—to be blessed with that touch of insanity needed to complete this crazy feat (again and again), but above all—to have such amazing, supportive people in my life.

Getting to the Start Line

Nine years after that first Ironman distance race in Atlantic City, I would be getting ready for my tenth and final Ironman distance race on September 11th, 2022, in Madison, Wisconsin, in honor of 9/11 first responders.

In early August 2022, just one month before the big race, I did a half-Ironman tune-up race in Boulder, Colorado, to ensure I was physically and mentally on track. I felt good that entire day, despite a brutal Colorado sun and temperatures over 90 degrees, which caused fellow athletes to drop out left and right.

That race took me six hours and forty minutes to complete—forty minutes longer than when I did the same course and distance in 2018—but I crossed that finish line with my arms raised and my trademark IronCEO smile. More important than the physical endurance I gained from this Ironman 70.3 tune-up, I now had the confidence to face another full Ironman.

The last few weeks before an Ironman is called the taper period. It's time to dial back the training intensity, giving your mind and body time to rest. At this point, pushing hard will only hurt your race day chances. I flew to Madison on a Thursday to finish my preparations.

That year, the organizers decided to hold the Ironman 70.3 race on Saturday and the full Ironman event on Sunday. Madison was buzzing with athletes, spectators, running shoes, and beer all weekend.

The triathlon gods and the weather shined on the half-Ironman competitors on Saturday; it was a perfect race day. But the weather forecast for Sunday painted a different picture: rain would start Saturday night and continue all day Sunday into the evening, with peak temperatures in the low fifties.

Based on the gloomy weather forecast, I knew the race would challenge me. Still, in my mind, the outcome was never in doubt. I knew that, as long as I showed up in the first place and didn't overthink it, I would finish what I started.

It rained the entire day—hard, cold, brutal rain. In a normal year, the DNF rate for this course ranged between 5 and 10 percent. That year, more than 25 percent of competitors either decided against racing or dropped out after starting.

Even after nine Ironman distance finishes, I knew it was perfectly normal to feel jitters when I thought about the magnitude of this feat.

"Why the hell am I doing this again?" was, admittedly, a common pre-race thought, even for this self-proclaimed IronCEO. My anxiety levels felt higher than usual as I stood in the mud for twenty minutes on the grassy shore, waiting to enter Lake Monona on that cold, wet, dreary day. My confidence wavered as I realized that, now at age sixty, I had never raced in such miserable, challenging conditions.

Next, I proceeded to do exactly what you're not supposed to do: I began worrying about every possible variable, drawback, and potential disaster. How would road conditions look on the bike course? What if I crashed? How would my body react to the cold and wet? *If I don't stay warm*, I thought, *I'll be toast*.

Hearing the Star-Spangled Banner, followed by the explosive race gun, aroused my energy and adrenaline, but did not calm my nerves. Still, the doubts washed away when I entered the comparatively warm lake water.

No turning back now; the race was on.

Surf to Turf

That surprisingly soothing 2.4-mile swim would be the most comfortable I'd feel all day. The chop wasn't bad enough to affect my stroke, and the lack of sun made sighting the course a breeze.

The mind stops playing games when fully occupied. It now had a job to do: figure out how to survive each next second of the following sixteen hours—all the way to another Ironman finish line.

I swam under the banner one hour and forty-one minutes later, indicating the swim finish. After slogging through the mud, volunteers stripped my wetsuits. Next, I ran up a massive ramp on the helix of the parking lot, past a raucous crowd, to enter the convention center and follow the signs for the first transition area, T1.

There, men and women, in separate areas, grabbed their numbered gear bags and put on their bike shoes, helmets, and layers of rain clothes. Next, we all hurried out the exit doors and ran to the bike racks, where 1,500 bikes awaited riders.

The time taken to transition from swim to bike, then later from bike to run, all counted toward my overall finishing time. I tried to be efficient, but the crowded, frenzied logistics of grabbing my gear bag, changing, and getting back on course—let's just say—was not my strong suit. It took more than seventeen minutes to get through T1 and back on the course, easily double my average. Seven hours later, my T2 transition time would be even worse.

Before riding my bike down the exit ramp, I grabbed a quick kiss from my biggest fan, my wife, whom I affectionately nicknamed the "Iron Sherpa" for her dutiful and loving support. She'd been waiting and watching all day as I set sail for that wet, rainy, nasty ride. During moments like these, I can't explain how much Beth encourages and energizes me. Triathlon may be a solitary sport, but the love and support of this beautiful woman, throughout the years, has given me so much courage and strength.

But this was no time for romantic reflections. I still had 112 miles to bike and a marathon to run!

Normally, after stripping off your wetsuit, your triathlon kit quickly dries in the sun, and you wear it for the rest of the day. But that day, with the goal of staying as warm and dry as possible, I'd planned for a full clothing change at each transition. Plenty of racers, from professional triathletes to amateurs, brought rain gear, or at the very least, makeshift rain jackets from garbage bags. With constant rain from early morning to well past midnight, I'm afraid those garbage bags did them little good and mainly got in the way, and I'm sure they paid for their mistake later.

I rode the wet roads with a simple rain jacket and fingerless hobo gloves improvised from bike socks with cutouts for my fingers. Finally, I'd tucked a pair of sunglasses into my pocket. Why the shades? Because preparation and optimism were both keys to success. *What if the sun came out?* This proved to be wishful thinking as the deluge persisted.

Still, much like the swim, riding my bike calmed my nerves. A confident cyclist and competent bike handler, I found I could handle the rain. While plenty wet, the tarmac remained free from puddles and car grease. As long as the pedals turned and wheels spun, I could channel these challenges through my usual adrenaline rush to pump out my favorite part of any triathlon.

It was easy to stay in what I call my "Zone Two Zen"—until the first sharp turn. Carbon wheels, rain, and rim brakes are not a good combination. At every curve, I had to anticipate the turn and squeeze the brakes until my fingers bled. This increased my focus and forced me to check my speed, preventing me from overcooking the racecourse.

The rain jacket worked, and staying in the aero position and keeping my head down would help me avoid rain spikes in my eyes. If I could have worn my sunglasses, they would have ironically helped keep the rain out of my eyes. Every fast descent became a delicate balancing act that required that I pick up my head and chest to maintain a clear field of vision.

The main secret to staying warm on a bike, of course, was just to keep pedaling. I pedaled hard, both up and down hills. Fortunately, my lungs and quads could handle short, punchy climbs—because there were many. I passed one rider who said it felt like Groundhog Day because the color of the sky, temperature, and precipitation stayed drearily constant all day.

I had to agree. By that point, time had lost all meaning. I rarely glanced at my bike computer to check the elapsed time or speed. I needed to stay in the moment and keep moving. To track distance, I noted the passing of each 10-mile marker on the road, trusting my pace would get me to the finish line, where I would, once again, hear the announcer chant: "You are an Ironman!"

Given my bike's fancy electronic derailleur with push-button gear shifting, shifting gears normally took no effort at all. But this time I still struggled to maintain smooth control as my gloves had soaked through, leaving my fingers numb and stiff. Not only that, but my bike computer failed after mile 100 due to a drained battery. Still, my bike and I were gamers for all 112 miles.

Finally, I cruised up the helix into a volunteer bike catcher's warm, waiting arms. After racking my bike, the catcher pointed me toward my running gear bag and changing area. I took a moment to appreciate this army of local volunteers. With such a complex organism of trucks, equipment, gear, and logistics, these individuals truly make race day possible.

I finished that hilly bike course in a slow but manageable seven hours and forty-three minutes. While I'm no speed demon, on a dry day where I wouldn't need to check my speed, I'd have easily reduced my biking time by an hour.

The Final Leg

I can only conclude that Ironman creators were somewhat sadistic when establishing the distances for each race segment. While I can handle a two-mile swim and a 100-mile bike run, it's always the last 600 meters of swimming and twelve miles of cycling when I question my sanity. The ensuing run is truly torturous—for basically the entire 26.2 miles.

Thankfully, the T1 and T2 transition areas were inside big convention center areas. At this second and final transition point, I started to realize just how cold I was. My fingers were so numb that I could not unclip my helmet strap without assistance. I also needed help peeling off my wet bike clothing in the changing room. I took almost thirty minutes to warm up, change clothes, and make another bathroom stop. I saw my fellow competitors shivering—but I also saw them passionate and determined to get on with the show. That energy from other athletes, volunteers, and spectators kept me going, as always.

Done right, the Ironman race could become a rolling meditation; the longer I went, the more I settled into that calm, reflective zone inside my head. The bike saddle felt not unlike a good therapist's couch, offering time and a safe place for introspection. There, I could reflect on my life's journey and process the many memories and emotions that bubbled up. There was certainly a lot on my mind during this day of remembrance on September 11.

Compared to that, however, the run felt small and contracted, like solitary confinement in a straitjacket. That may sound harsh, but my only point is that—instead of the vast, imaginative mental afforded by my bike ride—my running vision narrowed to a pinhole. I only thought about putting one foot in front of the other. I remember that run, including intermittent chats with strangers, but I can't remember thinking about anything aside from making every step count. I liked this place too. Clearing my mind of extraneous matters and returning to simply breathing, pumping my legs, and surviving the course felt therapeutic.

Still, the time for psychoanalysis was over; I had a job to finish. I may have mastered the mindset to become an Ironman, but my legs still needed to run this damn marathon. When the run started on the helix down ramp, my first mile clocked in at a blazing eleven minutes and twenty-one seconds. My legs and feet felt fine so far. After several twelve to thirteen-minute miles, I settled into my usual running routine.

I call this my "Ironman shuffle"—a slow, continuous fourteen-minute-mile jog. I could see other athletes walking as fast as my supposed running pace. Unlike past races, I barely stopped to walk between aid stations, able to eat and drink as I shuffled along without much discomfort.

I had long since surrendered to the wetness, but at least running kept my body warmer than biking. During runs, I'm a pack rat, carrying all my nutrition and a hand bottle of my secret energy drink concoction. My biggest running asset is my iron-like stomach. I can keep gobbling calories to stay strong. My only mistake was carrying a two-pound bag of various salt-covered gummies, which I'd occasionally—reluctantly—jettison to lighten my load.

On the edges of my tunnel vision, I heard the wonderful volunteers and spectators who shivered through the cold, dark, and wet night to cheer us on. I fed off this energy, particularly from my Iron Sherpa; her smiles and hugs soothed me each time like warm chicken broth.

Finally, I cruised into the Madison downtown area, where the faster athletes—those who had already run both laps—could veer left for the finish chute. The double-lap run course always teased runners with a premature sight of the finish line. Turning right for that second, final, 13.1-mile lap was the cruelest moment of any Ironman race.

Luckily, my Iron Sherpa was there for more kisses, hugs, and encouragement. With no chance of finishing in a podium position for my age group or qualifying for the Ironman World Championship in Kona, Hawaii, I could afford the extra time to take selfies with my wife in front of the illuminated Wisconsin capitol dome.

Then, as that midnight deadline closed in, I set out into the lonely darkness of lap two, to close out what would soon become my final Ironman finish. While the weather lessened their numbers, the streets were still lined with spectators and families cheering, clapping, and clanging cowbells to push me forward. I saw those last 13.1 miles strictly as a math equation, simply counting down the miles from 13.1 to zero. This was when my confidence rose, and I told myself: *Alex, you are going to do it.*

I faced an additional variable this time around. My average swim, bike, and run splits usually put me into the fifteenth-hour finishing chute. However, until that final lap, I'd neglected to mentally account for the extra-long transition times and the dilly-dallying with my wife.

My gut told me I had until midnight to finish this Ironman (even though my brain secretly knew I had seventeen hours from my swim start time, which in my case would be thirty minutes past midnight). I listened to my gut and willed myself to keep up my pace along this long, dark, and lonely section of the run course alongside Lake Mendota with gravel, mud, deep puddles, and wind—but thankfully no lions, tigers, or bears. I could grind out the final miles in relative happiness and comfort. I was going to finish this Ironman.

One of my favorite Ironman sayings is that only the last mile counts. Whether you race 50 or 139.6 miles, you cannot call yourself Ironman. I try to make that last mile my best, so I always set the same three goals for every Ironman race: 1. Finish the race, 2. Run strong through into the finish chute, and 3. Always cross the finish line with a smile.

Since I wasn't worried much about how fast I finished each leg or where I placed overall, I maintained the mental and physical ability to not just endure but also enjoy and even cherish, every moment of this arduous event.

I stopped to kiss Beth one last time, with only 100 yards remaining before I hit the finishing chute. Then, I zipped up my custom imprinted IronCEO Triathlon suit and removed excess rain gear to ensure I looked like a pro crossing the finish line.

During those magical last 100 yards, the pain and darkness disappeared. Pure adrenaline, mixed with cheers from the crowd propelled my tired feet forward—along with the pride of knowing I was about to achieve something so epically challenging that only my fellow racers and closest loved ones could appreciate what it took to get here.

With 50 yards remaining, the emotions of 9/11 hit me in full force. To celebrate my beloved hometown and cheer for those who could no longer be heard, I started yelling, "New York! New York!"

Ten yards left. With the finishing chute in front of me, I slowed down to soak in the noise, bright lights, music, and ceremony. I began scanning the crowd for Mike Reilly, the official "Voice of Ironman." It would not be official until this man uttered the famous words that will forever mark my accomplishment: "Alex Cooper, The IronCEO—you are an Ironman!"

With that, I crossed the finish line with both hands in the air and all ten fingers pointing to the sky—to honor all the heroes of 9/11 and celebrate my ten Ironman finishes. I expected a flood of emotion and tears. Instead, there was only joy and calm. One volunteer wrapped me in a blanket to warm me up, while another placed a "finisher" medal around my rain-soaked neck.

Next, I searched the crowd for Beth, my soulmate, life companion, and biggest supporter. I gave her a big wet hug and thanked her for staying out in the miserable cold rain for more than sixteen hours.

I had one final task before putting this race into the books. I knew Mike Reilly was set to retire. Since this marked one of his last races as the Voice of Ironman, I trotted over to personally shake his hand, thank him, and wish him well. Then I gave him a new "IronCEO" trucker hat I'd carried in my back pocket for the last 26.2 miles. When I'd bumped into Mike early at the swim start and told him I had a retirement gift for him at the finish line, he said he preferred cash. (Sorry, Mike.)

That concluded my tenth and final Ironman finish. While it may have been my slowest race, I'd faced by far the most challenging weather conditions and proven to myself that, at sixty years old, I still had what it took to endure the race.

True Endurance

Endurance happens when you build the mental skills to face untold hardship, suffering, and pain. You don't have to race an Ironman, run a marathon, or even jog a 5k to achieve this.

But you do have to prove, through courage and consistency, that you can show up for yourself and commit to your goals.

Still, there's nothing like Ironman to test this commitment to showing up and finishing strong. Crossing even one Ironman finish line is a life-changing experience. Suddenly, even huge challenges feel small and unimpressive as you gain the confidence and resilience to face any failure or adversity.

When I started racing triathlons, I certainly set goals and expectations. I wanted to improve from race to race and from year to year. After a while, I stopped thinking about them as races because where and when I finished no longer mattered. Letting go of results made all the difference, freeing me to experience the joy of each moment.

It may sound insane that a 140.6-mile exertion is my happy place, but that's the gift of endurance training. To see what you're truly capable of, endurance must first become a boring, daily habit. One that involves realistic expectations, pacing, and regular rest to recover and rejuvenate the mind and body. The real aim of endurance training is not just to become better athletes, but also better leaders, parents, partners, neighbors, and human beings—by building both mental and emotional resilience.

None of this happens overnight. It requires daily investments of time and effort to develop and reinforce. Endurance may take years to build, and its surface gains can be lost in a matter of weeks. But in the end, endurance happens when you combine a consistent commitment to your goals with pure passion.

So where did my passion come from? What made me believe I had the right stuff to compete in such an audacious endeavor?

As I said, the first—and by far, most important—step is to dare to sign up in the first place. Next, you must commit to getting to the start line. This means being willing to fail, if it comes to that. I never expected to fail and haven't yet, but I always accepted the risk—and I've seen firsthand how fear of failure can stop people from even trying.

After dipping my toes in the Ironman waters, I learned it can be a sport for regular guys like me. Sure, you needed a wetsuit, a decent bike, and running shoes. But the most essential ingredient is not talent or athletic prowess. Success or failure, either one, has everything to do with mindset. Cliche as it may seem, you just needed to believe in yourself—and I did.

Can you show up, commit, and accept possible failure, while believing in your ability to succeed? If so, you can become an Ironman too.

Checking all these boxes doesn't mean you won't face challenges and adversity while running the race. But true endurance means having the confidence and perseverance to keep going anyway. To push into the next stroke, pedal, or step, no matter how you feel, takes a mental fortitude far surpassing any physical training.

Endurance takes many forms. I've endured the ups and downs of building and helming three tech startups. I also endured tragedies, including the loss of both parents, the death of my girlfriend Jill, and the terrorist attacks on the World Trade Center on 9/11. Even without racing an Ironman, I would have found the resilience and fortitude to overcome my losses, but I wouldn't have been the same.

Unless you're truly sadistic, nobody asks for suffering. Still, it finds us, each and every one. The strength to endure lies within us all; it comes from within. Without Ironman, I still would have found the resilience and fortitude to overcome my obstacles and losses. However, in pushing myself past what I'd ever imagined possible, I gave myself the courage and conviction to conquer any challenge, including my life-changing diagnosis.

Ironman represented more than just a physical or mental challenge for me. It was my life's calling. Being a ten-time Ironman finisher transformed me. Above all, it taught me that true endurance meant focusing on the preparation and journey rather than the result.

Chapter 12
Signs From Above

March 14, 2023: Radiation begins

Six weeks after my first surgery, I met the new frontline ranks of my battle with cancer. After the surgeon's scalpel, chemotherapy and radiation would be the next weapons of choice.

That first meeting with the oncologist and radiologist came about two weeks before I would drop my PT and OT visits to focus on my personal brand of physical therapy. At that point, I'd already been walking and cycling in my Pain Cave, and I'd just negotiated my return to skiing and swimming. That might help explain why the first visit with my new doctors felt so emotional. I was getting back into the groove of my IronCEO regimen, and I didn't yet know whether the famously brutal side effects of radiation stood to take that away.

This hospital visit also reminded me that although my physical and mental scars from the surgery were healing, the cancer was still in me. It would be another four months before my next MRI, the first critical marker for measuring progress.

Meanwhile, the next line of defense would be *offense*—against cancer, but also against my system generally. Chemo and radiation therapies aren't exactly known for their precision targeting; they tend to bring on extreme general fatigue, nausea, hair loss, headaches, and more.

I could not escape feelings of anxiety and doubt as Beth and I waited to greet the new team of doctors now in charge of my care. I struggled at times to understand the oncologist's delivery and absorb the content of his words. Still, the professionalism of the team eventually put me at ease, as did my immediate rapport with my radiologist.

Another IronCEO mindset principle I both practiced and preached is the notion that *everything you have done has led you to this moment*. Above all, it's a mindset shift, a reframing of your mental storyline. Anytime you feel in over your head, especially when starting a new position or taking a business risk, you can always mine your past for gold—for those nuggets of experience or transferable skills that make you the perfect match for any next challenge at hand.

I offer this as pragmatic advice to peers and mentees preparing their resumes or interviewing for a new job. Whether or not you can check off every qualification on the job description, you can figure out how your past has prepared you to tackle this next obstacle or opportunity.

It's not wishful thinking exactly, more a combination of optimism and decisiveness. I've learned to consciously choose confidence by focusing on the positive—on how my unique set of life experiences has led me to every new moment at hand.

By the time I started chemo and radiation, I'd had a lot of practice with the preparedness principle, but I wholeheartedly believed—and still believe—that every challenge, achievement, and accomplishment has strengthened me for my battle with cancer.

Still, to maintain this positive mindset, I wanted to guard against too much information about probabilities and outcomes. So, at the outset of this important visit, I made that clear.

"I'm not interested in statistics," I told them. "My experience with cancer is mine alone, and so is my ability to fight it, so please don't pile on the data or focus on potential negative outcomes. Just tell me what we need to do next."

Just like with Ironman competitions, the numbers didn't matter. I didn't compare race times or rankings, so why should I care about medical statistics or points on some bell curve chart? Only one set of numbers and information mattered: my own.

Just as your unique set of experiences prepares you to face each new moment, they also determine your own, individual outcomes. You can't compare your past journey to anyone else's or use other people's data to predict your future.

Daily Assaults

I may have gone in with an individualistic mindset, but my next treatment plan followed an established standardized regimen. For six weeks, I would take an oral chemo pill every day and receive radiation on weekdays to reduce the tumor and other precancerous potential hot spots in my brain. I was warned that these daily assaults on cancer might come with some collateral damage.

The doctors didn't hold back. I could expect side effects like nausea, loss of appetite, and vomiting; serious fatigue, aches and pains, itchiness, and hair loss. Luckily, that last part didn't apply to me since I was already bald.

Fortunately, my daily radiation sessions took place at a satellite medical facility only a five-minute walk from my house. A week before the first treatment, I met the nursing and radiology team and prepared an unusual theatrical prop: a mask of my face and head they would use to clamp my head into a fixed position to better target my tumor. To create the mold for this mask, they layered warm, wet sheets of plaster over my face and then allowed them to dry in place. The resulting mask made me look like the spooky anti-hero in *The Phantom of the Opera.*

Receiving daily radiation treatment went way smoother than expected. Unlike the noisy, confining MRI and CAT scan contraptions, radiation sessions felt quick and easy. I would lay on a flat table as a technician placed the mask over my head and clamped me into a (surprisingly comfortable) position. Finally, the machine would move around me and work its magic.

I appreciated having room to breathe and relative peace and quiet. Best of all, the technician could pipe music into the treatment room. Then, after ten minutes and a couple of Bruce Springsteen classics—by request, of course—the machine stopped and the table raised. After the tech removed my phantom mask, I was free to go.

Each morning, I'd walk to my 8:30 a.m. appointment and get out by 8:50 a.m. After that, I could do whatever I pleased with the rest of the day. The central advice the radiology team gave me was: "Keep active and avoid being sedentary, even when feeling fatigued."

To that, I laughed. "Oh, don't worry about me," I said. "That won't be a problem." To keep moving had always been my core mantra and mandate. It would serve me well here, too. Throughout the next month and a half, I maintained my workout goals, my IronCEO mindset, and—mercifully—relatively good outcomes.

To cut the suspense, I somehow managed to evade the most common side effects of digestive misery, pain, and exhaustion. Sure, I felt more tired than usual, and I dealt with occasional headaches, but compared to the physical gauntlet of 140-mile Ironman races, I felt fine. I largely chalked this up to my past physical conditioning and my IronCEO mindset of confident preparedness.

That said, athletic ability and attitude alone won't always spare patients from the horrible side effects of chemo and radiation. I knew I was fortunate to get off so easy, and I didn't want to take that for granted. Sometimes, while clamped into my mask, listening to familiar Springsteen tunes, and planning my afternoon ride, swim, or run, I'd silently—humbly—give thanks to whatever angels, karma, or sheer dumb luck might be on my side.

Ski Therapy

Beth had restored my outdoor biking privileges, albeit with restrictions. Now I had a full arsenal of physical activities to occupy me: walking, cycling, running, yoga, swimming, and even skiing. In the end, neither the radiation nor the chemo slowed me down much. Day by day, I would pick my pleasure and, weather permitting, get outside to exercise in the brisk March sun. On days when it rained, snowed, or simply proved too cold, I'd head to the Pain Cave trainer. Before long, my runs increased to forty-five to sixty minutes, and my bike rides to two hours. Since exercise intensity depended on a person's overall fitness and ability, I knew I wasn't overtaxing my system.

I spent my most joyous days skiing on the slopes. I skied three days before my surgery and mere weeks after being discharged. I'm not sure what my doctors thought about my extreme activity levels. Aside from that first day Beth and I announced I would start skiing again, we had yet to ask them.

After returning to the slopes, I never skied alone. I had a posse of ski buddies, including my kids. They would take turns driving me up to the mountains and keep a watchful eye on their wounded warrior.

Before my illness, my ski companions adorned me with the nickname "Bunny," a reference to those Duracell Energizer commercials of the late 1980s. I've never been the fastest or most graceful skier, but I've always had the benefit of boundless energy. The cancer treatments only slightly tempered my energy. Out of caution—and Beth's insistence—I agreed to the concession of avoiding trees and challenging terrains.

Happy Hour Fridays

A few weeks in, I switched my Friday radiology treatments to 3 p.m. This way, I could hit the slopes until 1 p.m., then strip off my gear, and head back with my ski chauffeur for a few zaps on my skull—which I soon took to calling "Happy Hour Friday."

This tight schedule meant I cut it close some days, but I never missed a radiation appointment. I was working on "Alex Time," which meant squeezing as much as I possibly could into each 24-hour day.

This frenetic schedule admittedly weighed on me at times. On one particular Happy Hour Friday, I began second-guessing my training standards. Then, as the radiology technician lowered me into position for my treatment, he said, "Alex, you are a wild man—and I mean that in the best possible way."

That was all the validation I needed to lean into my goals. Sometimes, what others considered madness felt like pure sanity to me.

The cherry on top of my Happy Hour Friday cocktails, of course, was my hand-picked musical playlist. The team knew about my bottomless fandom for Bruce Springsteen. I grew up in Queens, New York, but I spent more than 30 years raising my family in New Jersey. As such, I'm the quintessential cliche of a Jersey guy and a Springsteen nut.

Before long, blasting Springsteen during Happy Hour Fridays was not a request; it was an assumption.

Since those early lunch-period retreats to the record player at my high school library, Bruce Springsteen always set the soundtrack to my life. I have seen him play live more than fifty times over the years. Bruce even showed up after I received the call informing me of my mother's death. Within an hour of hanging up the phone, the radio played a rare, somber Springsteen song, 'Streets of Philadelphia." In its relatable melancholy, the song felt like recognition, providing a musical salve for the pain.

As I lay clamped in my mask, listening to Springsteen, my mind wandered about twenty years into the past, back to the summer of 2002, when I'd traveled to Lake Placid in upstate New York's Adirondack Mountains to bring my then-twelve-year-old son to hockey camp.

Unbeknownst to me, "the Boss" himself was also visiting Lake Placid that summer in a fatherly role, to see his daughter compete in a horse show. On a friend's recommendation, I took Evan to a bar and grill called Lisa G's for dinner—but when we arrived, the manager came out to apologize and explain that the restaurant could not accept more guests due to a special party inside.

Curious, I asked who the party was for and learned it was none other than my musical idol, Bruce Springsteen. Naturally, the only possible next step was to half-charm, half-force my way inside, to at least try to say hello.

Once I slipped past the restaurant's defenses, I managed to approach Bruce—and to his credit, he could not have been more gracious about my unexpected interruption.

"I just have something quick to share, if you don't mind," I explained.

Before Bruce (or his security team) could say *no*, I politely introduced him to Evan, who was born just a year before the arrival of Springsteen's own firstborn son—whom he also named Evan. I went on to quickly explain that a couple years later, my first wife and I welcomed our daughter, Jessica, also born shortly before the birth of Springsteen's daughter, who also—incredibly—shared *her* name.

Some might call this a coincidence, but to me, life's uncommon synchronicities feel like more than chance. They feel like reminders of our deep human connections, not just to our loved ones, but also to strangers we might meet along the way, or even artists whose musical gifts uplift us or ease our sorrows.

While the spirit to battle cancer comes from within, Springsteen's boost of energy and inspiration sure helped keep me in fighting form.

The nurse's voice cut through my reverie and the energizing lyrics of *Thunder Road*.

"Are you experiencing any side effects?"

"No."

'Do you have any questions?'

"No." Everything I've experienced in life has prepared me for this moment. I got this.

Chance Encounters

Before my brain surgery, the physical deficit I'd developed on my right side challenged my ability to hold a razor or clippers to properly shave my balding head. Beth had dutifully stepped in to assume the barber duties—until the surgical scar intimidated her enough to call in the pros.

I Googled my way to the closest neighborhood barbershop. When I plopped down in the comfy barber's chair the following Wednesday at noon, I settled in, not expecting anything other than a quick cut and some conversation.

Barbershops were made for extroverts like me. I loved shooting the breeze. To me, even idle chat and gossip served a purpose, whether checking out a new sales prospect at work or just forming new connections with neighbors.

My new barber went right to work, surveying my scalp to determine the appropriate blade length. Meanwhile, I launched into conversation, asking if his slight accent was Russian.

The backstory he told hit me right between the eyes. His family originally hailed from the former Soviet Union. Like my mother and father, they were Jewish and immigrated to the U.S. from Kazakhstan. And like me, he'd grown up in Queens, New York—in my very own childhood neighborhood of Forest Hills.

"A landsman!" I proclaimed, using the translation for the Yiddish word describing a fellow Jew who shares your same district or town of origin.

Our parallel universes drew closer when I mentioned that, after growing tired of my mother always cutting my hair, I started going around the corner of Queens Boulevard to our Italian-owned barbershop. There, the proprietor—"Sabino himself," I recalled fondly—cut my hair for most of my teenage years. To this, my new landsman just smiled and asked if I knew his father, too. It turned out, his dad had also worked for years, cutting hair at Sabino's Barber Shop.

This unlikely synchronicity seemed to set off cosmic sparks between us. I excitedly explained that my mother had also immigrated to Forest Hills in Queens, from Eastern Europe after surviving the Holocaust. She'd worked as a manicurist in a salon just three doors from Mr. Sabino's Barbershop.

This unexpected connection to my mother felt like a sign from above, energizing me to endure the rest of my treatment and recommit to living my life the best way I knew how: accepting challenges and forging connections—with loved ones, acquaintances, and even strangers—wherever I could find them.

Grand Finale

Around that same time, I received an incredible surprise from a college friend.

I had known Bruce Springsteen was scheduled to perform at Denver's Ball Arena on March 22, 2023—hell, I'd even bookmarked the date in advance, feeling somehow sure I'd make the show, despite the cutthroat competition for tickets. As the date came closer, though, I resigned myself to possibly missing the concert, not feeling up to my usual cunning street hunt for pre-show scalpers.

Little did I know that my college friend, Gard, who had accompanied me to Springsteen concerts decades before, managed to get in touch with someone from the Springsteen Organization. His initial goal was to have them convince Bruce to record a personal message to cheer me up and inspire me. What I got instead was much more special: VIP tickets to the show!

I'll never forget that concert. Our seats put us as front and center as you can get while still getting to sit throughout the long show. Bruce opened the show with "No Surrender," one of my all-time favorite anthems, and after an incredible 26-song setlist, he closed with "See You in My Dreams."

This newer Springsteen song reflected on life's many changes and the challenges of getting older, including having to grieve the loss of bandmates and friends. As I listened, I thought about my own experiences with love, loss, and aging, as well as my current situation. Every moment of sacrifice or glory, every heartfelt connection and relationship in life—eventually turning everything into memories, those reminders of love tucked away like divine gifts from above.

After hearing this moving finale, I realized that, even without the cancer, I would have chosen to make this perfectly bittersweet performance my last Springsteen show. The feeling hit just like that premonition I felt before racing my tenth and final Ironman. I'll always cherish Bruce's musical gifts, but every chapter runs its course. While you can't recreate the past, you can know when to gather your memories and experiences and move on to the next step of the journey.

Back to the Races

The best compliment you can receive from your medical team is that you're a boring patient. I heard this praise from the ICU nurses after my surgery. Same story for my weekly check-ins with the nurse and doctor in the Radiology Center.

My blood pressure, heart rate, and—most importantly—red and white cell blood kept coming back normal. Each week, the nurse asked the same two questions, and each week I shook my head: No side effects. No questions. All good.

Instead of discussing symptoms and medical needs, I used the doctors' and nurses' time to dole out advice on endurance sports. The nurse had organized a team of runners from the radiology group to run the Denver Colfax half marathon on May 20, 2023, to raise money for a worthy charity. She was approximately my age, but not an avid runner or athlete. To build herself up to the appropriate mileage, she'd been training with a running group.

I listened to her training routine, then spewed my wisdom before waiting to ask if she wanted advice. I told her to get used to the pounding on her feet. She needed to run more on pavement instead of just on a treadmill. In place of the grimace I expected (and deserved), the nurse smiled patiently and thanked me.

My other weekly visit—with my radiation oncology doctor—presented a similar opportunity to flex my coaching muscles. Though still nursing a knee injury, the attending radiation oncologist also hoped to run the Colfax half-marathon. An aspiring triathlete himself, he eagerly asked about my triathlon experience.

Thanks to my encouragement, if not outright proselytizing, my radiologist signed up to race an Ironman 70.3 triathlon. This heartened me almost more than my own slow but steady progress. Whether on the race course, in the office, or in my personal life, empowering others to achieve their goals and dreams gives me a thrill like nothing else. I still recall, during my second full marathon in Boulder, Colorado, when a friend of mine nearly psyched himself out. When I saw him later during the race, he was contemplating throwing in the towel. I slowed down to walk with him, encouraging him to stay in the race and just focus on each next step. It worked! Not only did he start running again, but he even finished before me. I count this vicarious win among my racing career highlights.

I began pondering a seemingly crazy notion. What if I joined the radiology running team to toe the line for the Colfax race? If 13.1 miles was too much, a simultaneous 10-mile race would begin at the same time and start line.

If you plant a seed in my brain, cancer-ridden or not, it will grow. My goal-driven IronCEO mindset suddenly needed the group challenge to add to my now-empty race calendar.

I had no illusions about recapturing my pre-treatment athletic stats. At that point, my legs felt leaden when I ran and I knew I might spend more of that race walking than ever before. My desire to race again had more to do with challenging myself and connecting to others through competitive camaraderie.

Mainly I needed a boost to my confidence. On days when I skied more challenging terrains with friends or pushed myself hard on bike rides, doubts had begun creeping in. I'd start asking myself whether I was up to the rest of the course or ride—only to push through and regain my mojo after a few more miles or runs down the slopes. Despite my significantly reduced performance, the routine of daily exercise kept my

The Courage to Finish What You Started

life feeling normal, soothing my brain and soul as much as it strengthened my body.

During those six weeks of radiation therapy—when many patients found even everyday tasks like eating unbearably difficult—I felt grateful for my merciful lack of nausea, extreme fatigue, and other symptoms. Instead, I was able to slowly increase my mileage and even seriously entertain the idea of entering Denver's largest half and full-marathon event.

While I wasn't ready to commit just yet, I knew full well where this was heading. But first, I needed to complete the six full weeks of chemo and radiation to see how my body responded to the full treatment.

Next, I needed a relatively clean bill of health from my doctors before I could pin a running bib to my shorts on race day.

My final treatment came on April 10, 2023, after six weeks of daily chemo pills and thirty radiation treatments. I'd made it through a successful surgery and the gauntlet of chemotherapy and radiation treatments without a hiccup.

I had a month's "vacation" from hospitals, doctors, and therapists to rest, recover, and regain my strength. I now had no excuse not to ramp up my training for the half marathon.

A Stranger's Smile

After that month's reprieve, I would also face my first postoperative MRI. During the six weeks of treatment, I'd tried not to think about outcomes. Still, every small headache, clumsy move, or scatterbrained moment of forgetfulness made me wonder if the cancer had rebounded. Overall, my energy levels hadn't changed much since starting my radiation and chemo treatments, but doubts still crept in.

On the morning of May 11, less than two weeks before the Colfax half marathon, I headed to the hospital for my 6:30 a.m. MRI appointment. I decided to take an Uber on my own, so Beth could sleep in. She would join me later that morning to meet with our oncology doctor for the results.

I received my first positive sign after hopping in a bright red Uber car. I'm not superstitious, but I do believe in good omens—that the right signals can appear at key times. The morning of my MRI, I received one loud and clear.

My Uber driver emanated good energy from a bright, radiant smile that filled his face. He sensed right away that I was a talker open to connecting. As always, I immediately launched into a conversation, asking the driver questions and learning about his fascinating heritage. Born in West Africa to a Jamaican mother, he had lived in many different countries and continents.

From the destination I entered in the Uber app, he knew I was heading to the hospital. I don't remember how much I told him about my illness, but I do remember his encouragement.

"I feel sure you will receive good news today," he said shortly after I got in. I grinned in response and thanked him sincerely.

"The cheapest, most powerful gift you can give is a smile," he said later. He had a beaming, contagious smile of his own. We went on to talk about spirituality and religion, and I shared that, while I believed in a higher power and sense of spiritual connection among people, I wasn't too religious.

"I am," he replied before offering examples of times when prayer had worked for him. When we pulled up to the hospital entrance, I thanked him and shook his hand, feeling uplifted and hopeful.

Moment of Truth

I admittedly struggled a bit to maintain this upbeat mood as I walked past the clean, modern entryway of the CU Anschutz

Medical Center and into the darker, basement-level inpatient ward where my MRI machine waited.

I had to walk with my radiology technician past the same operating rooms where I'd laid my life and brain at the hands of a skillful surgeon only three months earlier. It felt creepy, like returning to the scene of the crime.

Despite these forebodings, I managed to settle my emotions and get into my pre-MRI zen-like mindset. I lay calmly on the bed and focused on mindful breaths while the whirring and chirping of that cacophonous multi-million machine captured pictures of my brain. The easygoing nature of my Missouri-born technician and our ensuing discussion about whether he was a Kansas City Royals or St. Louis Cardinals fan also helped calm my nerves until I could free myself from that chaotic, confining tube.

With the MRI and blood work completed, my wife and I headed to the neuro-oncology waiting room and braced ourselves to meet with the oncologist. We entered the examination room, and before discussing the results, he asked me the usual: how I felt and if I had additional questions.

Rather than giving my standard replies (*Feeling great! No questions here!*), I paused.

This time, I had plenty of questions about what would come next—but I'd also been warned not to expect significant news about my prognosis during this consult. I'd heard from my team that MRI results were infamously "noisy" at this point, meaning that it would be difficult to determine just how much, if at all, the cancer had grown.

I wanted to ask about immunotherapy clinical trials I'd started reading about, as a potential supplement or alternative to the next treatment regimen: an increasingly higher chemo pill dose for five consecutive days every four to five weeks.

Finally, no matter the results of this or future MRIs, I was well aware of the cold, hard reality of my disease; at some point, the tumor would grow again. I needed to remain positive, but I knew one positive MRI result would not change my destiny.

I took a deep breath before peppering the doctor with questions. Then, I steeled myself to hear the results of that morning's MRI.

My doctor seemed pleased—almost nonchalant—when reporting his findings. He informed us I was not a good candidate for any trials because my cancer had neither grown at the original tumor site nor had it spread anywhere else in my brain. The surgery, radiation, and chemotherapy had done their job.

This wonderful news caught me by surprise. Doctors and nurse practitioners had repeatedly told us the initial post-op MRI might not indicate any progress.

"How are you so sure?" I bluntly asked.

"Well," he said, "it's true that this MRI is typically too noisy to confirm a patient's full status, but in your case, the images were clear and determinative: no new growth and no new tumors."

Beth and I walked out of that hospital with ear-to-ear smiles and sighs of relief. In my business career, I knew it was better to underpromise and overdeliver. Thankfully, my medical team subscribed to the same doctrine.

We drove home from the medical center, still trying to absorb the day's events and news. This meant we could remove the tentative status from our summer travel plans and move on with our lives—at least for now.

Mori Momento

Receiving a terminal diagnosis doesn't mean you stop living. Every day on this earth, we all move a bit closer to death. It's just a matter of perspective. As long as I can, I will choose to fully live each day rather than thinking I'm dying.

I started this chapter by talking about how my past experiences prepared me to endure cancer treatments that normally reduce patients to the sickbed. I do think my overall physical fitness, positive thinking, and history of punishing training habits helped. Before going into chemo and radiation, I'd long made a literal sport out of chasing pain and exhaustion through endurance conditioning.

That said, I also know that none of these previous efforts entitled me to any positive outcomes. My enduring energy and initial MRI triumph both humbled me and prompted me to reflect on the many gifts life has brought me, from a successful career and healthy family to those small, everyday reminders of grace and goodwill: something as simple as a coincidental connection with a landsman barber, a final performance from a lifelong musical hero—or a simple, heartfelt smile from an Uber driver.

In particular, the barbershop connection to my past helped me remember my mother's constant care and strength. In so many ways, my past feeds my spirit and prepares me for each new moment, and each new challenge to come.

I don't know if there are angels in heaven who send us signs. But I am positive that the spirit and soul of my mother and Sabino have looked after me since that day, from that final Bruce show through my daily chemo and radiation treatments.

Such moments of connection and synchronicity help restore my optimism and something like faith. To me, they suggest that, although life can sometimes appear senseless or unfair, there's an underlying order and interconnectivity to it all.

As I write this chapter's conclusion, we prepare for two of the most important and holy religious holidays on the Jewish calendar: Rosh Hashanah, the Jewish New Year's, and Yom Kippur, the Day of Atonement.

In particular, Yom Kippur reminds us to review the past year, wipe the slate clean by making amends, and set positive intentions for the upcoming year.

It's also a time to reflect on mortality. During the High Holiday liturgy, the rabbi reads the prayer "Unetaneh Tokef," which poses provocative rhetorical questions: "Who will live, and who will die? Who will live out their allotted time, and who will depart before their time?"

While—this year especially—I'm not exactly looking for further reminders of death, religion and philosophy both serve humanity by reminding us of all the ways that our lives prepare us for these ultimate ends: death and the legacies we leave behind.

Remembering these truths helps us gain perspective, as well as the wisdom and strength to prioritize what's important and make the right choices. Classical stoics like Marcus Aurelius praised the benefits of *mori memento*, or reminders of death. According to ancient wisdom, meditating on mortality even helps us find more joy in daily life.

Just as the past prepares us for the present and future, I believe that all of life's experiences have something to teach us, from tragic losses to heartfelt connections. The stories I've shared represent more than just friendly smiles and unlikely coincidences. Amid a real struggle to reconnect with my past and my faith through all these challenges, I've had to face my questions about life, death, and God.

I treasure all my life's many ups and downs—and I still believe it's all prepared me for whatever's coming next, all the way to the finish line. In the meantime, any and all signs from above are welcome.

Chapter 13
Not Done Yet

May 21, 2023: Colfax Half Marathon

The morning after my positive MRI report, Evan and I drove to our favorite ski resort to enjoy nearly 10 inches of fresh—but thick, cement-like—mountain snow. I attached climbing skins to the bottoms of my skies and skinned uphill for a lap as the pale dawn brightened overhead.

On reaching a suitable crest, I turned and squinted out over the glinting white slopes, lined in the distance with dark spruces or firs and setting off impossibly blue skies. I inhaled the chill of clean Rocky Mountain air, then tilted forward to catch that swift, sudden descent.

Zooming down snowy mountainsides always brings a hint of the childhood freedom of riding bikes. There's just something about leaning into gravity and harnessing its energy. It might seem scary at first—and for good reason. Especially when skiing, every beginner should expect a lot of falls. But by now, there's something comforting about the thrill of acceleration.

Since the surgery, I paid careful attention to my center of gravity and the coordination of my right arm, the latter of which still felt a bit off—but manageable. *So far, so good.* As an Ironman and seasoned skier, I knew my body like a musician knows his instrument. Its ability to recalibrate and adapt to discomforts and limitations comes from decades of endless repetitions. I relaxed into the descent, breathing in the pristine landscape around me, and let my thoughts sail by.

Before getting cancer, I'd described my IronCEO Mindset using words like consistency, dedication, and confidence. But lately, a new word has been at the center of my mind: *gratitude*.

Looking back at my life, I realized I'd never fully appreciated my blessings. Did any of us? It's almost impossible to stop and feel grateful as a distracted, energetic boy, a driven and hungry young man, or an even more distracted adult juggling executive duties with children and fitness goals and the million and one details and responsibilities of everyday life.

Buddhist philosophy reminds us that *now* is the only moment we have. Living in the past or worrying about the future, neither one helps much. Still, it's easy to spiral into fruitless time travel and miss the magic of everyday moments—of this moment.

Gratitude grounds us, even when it takes a retrospective view. Looking back with appreciation tends to humble us and neutralize regrets, turning even mistakes into lessons and opportunities for understanding, connection, and growth. It can alchemize even deeply painful experiences into unlikely gifts.

In a television interview I saw a few years back, Michael J. Fox discussed his decades-long journey with Parkinson's

Disease. He offered a one-sentence recipe for dealing with adversity:

"With gratitude, optimism is sustainable."

It takes optimism to start fitness training in the first place or to sign up for that first local 5K after you first start running—let alone attempt a marathon or triathlon event. As a ten-time Ironman, I knew how important it could be to *sustain* optimism over the long haul.

Since getting my diagnosis in early January, I'd mainly focused on *not dying* from cancer: surgery, chemo, radiation. As I slid through the snow that morning, I felt myself switch to a new paradigm: one of *living* with cancer.

My optimism always went hand-in-hand with the "Cooper Rule" of *just keep moving*. Taking decisive action required the confidence of a positive attitude and an innate excitement about life's possibilities. I couldn't have started three companies without optimism. Even as I navigated new limitations and taxing cancer treatments, I still felt the promise of each day to come.

That afternoon, after getting back from the slopes, I signed myself up for the Colfax half marathon on May 21, 2023, less than two weeks away. Feeling refreshed and ready to take on my next challenge, I called the hospital and managed to get my radiology nurse on the line.

"I'm joining your Colfax team!" I announced.

"Alex! That's so wonderful," she said, her tone elated but not surprised. "I know you'll get us all in gear and keep us motivated to get it done. You're such an inspiration!"

I smiled, but after hanging up, I gave a little sigh. I'd received similar feedback from friends, family, and other people I'd met during my cancer treatment, including my medical team. I could see how my ironclad dedication to activity goals and my upbeat mood in the face of brain cancer might help people think differently about their lives.

That said, I was just a guy coping with an awful situation the best way I knew how: by forging ahead and putting in the work with a smile. Whether in business or on an Ironman course, it's true that I've always gotten a rush out of boosting others up and helping them achieve their dreams. But I certainly didn't ask to be thrust into some heroic "cancer survivor" role.

This time, my motivation for running the Colfax half marathon was not so much to inspire others—but to give *myself* a boost. I craved that spice of challenge to season my life, and I was grateful as hell to still have the stomach for living on my terms.

I was still the IronCEO, and I wasn't done yet.

Living With Cancer

I've never been interested in blunt popular slogans like "Beat Cancer," "Fuck Cancer," or "Cancer Sucks." While I'm all for anything that motivates survivors to push on and people to donate to worthy causes, I needed a catchphrase that spoke to me.

Positive MRI or not, my cancer was still there, and it was never going away. That cloud would follow me down every snowy hill, on every run with my kids, and on every after-dinner stroll with Beth. The only variables I could still control were my reactions and emotions.

People like me—high-energy achievers drawn to extremes—tended to naturally thrive during crises. High stakes helped me focus, blocking out all background noise. But later, when the imminent threat passed, emotions could sometimes trickle (or flood) in. I'd maintained a good mental state for most of the past four months. Suddenly, the initial threat had downgraded to something more distant. We'd staved off trouble, for now.

With these three words, "living with cancer," I had my new mantra. I just needed to parse their meaning and determine the best way forward.

Ultimately, I knew this cancer would kill me. Instead of obsessing over defeating *cancer*, I needed to ensure that cancer would not defeat *me*. But how to go on each day living my best life? *How did I maintain gratitude and optimism even as I lost strength and stamina?*

Long used to reinventing myself, it was time to adjust my expectations and adapt.

Training for Colfax

After signing up, I had just ten days before my half marathon in the mile-high city. Ironman or not, you can't just show up and casually run 13.1 miles in Denver, where every step starts at 5,230 feet. Luckily, I'd been training, steadily increasing my mileage during and since my treatments.

Mindset was one ace in my hand. From experience, I knew I had what it took to show up on race day. If I could get to the starting line, finishing was a foregone conclusion, even if it meant walking for parts of the race.

Still, optimism and confidence only went so far. I had to do the work. Along with dedicated physical training, I needed to set realistic goals and expectations, based on ability—not ambition. All the preparation and positivity in the world could not make me run a marathon in three hours or throw a 95-mile-an-hour fastball.

That was where my second ace came in: my decades-long commitment to raising my base fitness level. I exercised every single day. Throughout the years—even outside of my so-called "triathlon season"—I'd still put in anywhere close to ten hours a week of aerobic training, weights, and yoga. The momentum built up from my lifetime of dedication made it easier to log similar hours of exercise following my first cancer surgery. My only concessions to cancer included reducing mileage and intensity of longer workouts, eliminating weights, and adding more walks and yoga sessions.

Starting in May, I'd raised my weekly mileage from eight miles to fourteen. My training was heading in the right direction—until I hit a bump on the road: I caught a virus.

After suffering through a two-week cough and nasal congestion, my wife passed her sickness to me. The congestion made breathing difficult, affecting both sleep and runs. I knew I could keep my aerobic fitness where it needed to be with biking alone but to give me the required confidence for this half marathon, I needed to do at least one ten-mile run before race day.

There were days when my legs felt like lead weights or the weather was too cold or wet for that long run or bike ride. Still, in the name of consistency, I would show up and muddle through, even if it was not my best. So, with a bad head and chest cold, less than two weeks before the race, I headed to my favorite route for extra motivation. With the way I felt, I'd need it. It was hard to say whether or not I'd be able to pump out ten miles—but there was only one way to find out.

I'm built for the long haul; the longer I run or bike, the better I tend to feel. Even after all these years, the first few miles often feel miserable. Runners often talk about "runner's high," but I just call it finding my groove. That day, it took about five miles before things started to feel easier. Even though I started the run with a cough and scratchy throat, my symptoms subsided as the miles passed.

During my six-week chemo and radiation sessions, I would sometimes get headaches, probably from swelling in my brain related to the surgery and radiation. But the headache would magically subside when I went outside for a run or bike ride. Adrenaline was a miracle drug that cured most daily ailments for me.

The main purpose of my ten-mile run was to boost my confidence. Running the Colfax Half would take two and a half hours at the pace I'd just finished ten miles. That was fine by me.

Start Line Jitters

The weekend before race week, I got in another seven-mile run. Then, still nursing a cough and sinus pressure, I did another four miles on the Wednesday before the race. Normally, I also ran a couple miles the day before a race just to get the blood flowing and warm up my legs. This time, I had a better idea.

I made the unorthodox move of heading to the mountains for a few hours of spring skiing. It was a beautiful day, and the fresh air and easy turns did my mind and legs good. I had all eternity to rest—or at least until I could no longer keep this up. Motion was my lotion, and I had to keep moving to feel good.

Race day finally arrived: Sunday, May 21. Since I lived two miles from the race, a 5:30 a.m. alarm gave me just enough time to get up and eat a quick bowl of oatmeal. On the course, I may be slow as molasses, but I raced like Usain Bolt when it came to getting to the starting line on time. I pinned on my race bib, put on an extra layer for the cool mountain air, and jumped on my bicycle for a quick warm-up ride to the park.

My daughter Jess, who had done numerous triathlons with me, knew my helter-skelter approach to race day well. Mainly because, with her precise organization, planning, and warmups, she was the exact opposite. While Jess's approach was the saner and more practical, I thrived amid chaos, typically arriving without adequate time to stretch, warm up, or even lower my heart rate from the scramble to get there on time. I may be a "type A" achiever, but the "speed of Alex'" always ensured that I typically slid breathless into my starting corral just as the National Anthem began.

True to form, I arrived at 6:25, with just minutes to spare, and sneaked into the corral labeled "C," despite being slated for Corral T. I wasn't trying to get a better position by queuing up with faster runners closer to the start; I was just running out of time.

Admittedly, my pre-event disorganization had drawbacks, whether I was showing up to a race or a big meeting. But staying calm among pandemonium remained among my biggest strengths. Because serious challenges tended not to fluster me, I could go with the flow and roll with the punches.

I took some deep breaths to find my zen and calm the butterflies in my stomach. If my legs weren't up to the full run, I knew I could always walk. But new pre-race emotions weighed on me as I wondered if this would be my last half marathon. I knew I could get to the finish line, but what if it marked the last one I'd ever cross?

Half Marathon

Finally, I hit the starting line, started my running watch, and raced. My last racing event had been the 9/11 Ironman Wisconsin. That day, I raced for fallen heroes and their families. While today, I was racing primarily for myself, I also wanted to do this for my family and friends.

Sure enough, within the first two miles, my doctor and nurse caught up with the rest of my participating radiation team. They immediately stopped me for a picture like some kind of celebrity. Their smiles and support put wind in my sails.

The running strides and miles came easy. While the crowd's energy always helped, my self-generated enthusiasm and joy drove my feet forward. Nothing expressed that happiness more than the never-ending smile on my face. Friends who had witnessed my races expressed shock that I never looked tired or distressed. Racing long distances truly made me happy. My legs grew weary, but regardless of the aches and fatigue, my IronCEO smile never disappeared.

It felt great to hear and feel the energy of 20,000 runners and multitudes of spectators on route that day. I finished the race in two hours and thirty-five minutes, close enough to my projected best time.

Loveland Triathlon

The relative ease with which I completed my half marathon in May gave me the confidence to add more events to my race calendar. I desperately wanted more goals and milestones to look forward to, so I signed up for my first postoperative triathlon, scheduled for June 24—along with my daughter.

For Jess, this Olympic-distance triathlon in the Loveland Colorado foothills would prove an easy training tune-up for her summer Ironman race schedule.

One thing I've always been deeply grateful for is the gift of participating in cycling, running, and triathlon races with my children. I'm proud that they've exceeded me in strength and speed, but mostly, I'm just glad to pass on things I love to my kids.

Rather than waking up before 4 a.m. to drive from Denver, Jess and I traveled to Loveland the afternoon before race day. That way, we could leisurely pick up our race packets, carb up at a local Thai restaurant, and settle into a hotel.

When our 5 a.m. alarm went off, I happily relinquished organizational duties to my talented and able daughter. Despite some highway detours, we got to the race with plenty of time to set up our bikes, prepare for the run transition, and put on wetsuits for a quick warm-up in Loveland Lake.

On race days, I like to say, "It's just another day in the office for the IronCEO." But this time, everything felt different. As my starting time approached, I tried to keep my emotions in check. Before leaving the transition area for the lakeside start, I took a moment to hug my daughter and shed a few tears of gratitude. Then, I put on my wetsuit and headed to the lake.

Jumping into the water felt like a baptism. My heart rate spiked from the cold and adrenaline before settling into a steady rhythm.

I purposely start at the back of my swim wave, or racing group. I never have a problem swimming the distance, but I move at the pace of a tortoise crossing the road, always finishing at the bottom 20th percentile. In the water, there's hardly any sound outside of breath and the soft splash of hands with each metered stroke. It's just me, racing against myself and the clock.

That day, surprisingly, I didn't feel the same pre-race jitters or doubts I'd felt before the half-marathon. My fitness level might never return to pre-cancer levels, but it was enough for an Olympic triathlon: an almost one-mile swim, followed by a nearly 25-mile bike ride, and just over six miles running.

That day, as I swam, the same bugbear thought popped up: *What if this is the last time I will ever do a triathlon?*

Knowing I needed to stop any downward spirals before they began. I pushed on through the water, suddenly realizing that I'd had exactly the same thought—not just before my Colfax half marathon—but also, unaccountably, before my final Ironman competition.

"I'm unsure if I'll race another . . ." suddenly those words took on a different tone in my mind. Not of defeat but of sudden, swelling gratitude. I realized with deep appreciation the truth of my words: "We don't get to choose our destiny or what day we will have glory or sacrifice. Sometimes, our destiny chooses us."

With that, I settled on my mantra for the rest of this race: gratitude.

There I was, on a beautiful course, doing what I loved. Why would I want to screw up this perfect moment by thinking about anything else? Just like that, I snapped back into the here and now.

My Happy Place

Back on dry land, after the swim, my mind and body returned to my happy place: my bicycle. Once my butt hit the saddle, the joy and relief of the second leg settled in.

That day's ride featured beautiful canyons, ranchlands, foothills, alpine lakes, snow-capped mountains—and pure awe. I have only experienced this transcendent emotion while biking, skiing, or hiking in the mountains.

All the cancer drugs and treatments available today may not have cured me. But the thrill and delight I experienced on this gorgeous bike ride were palliative, soothing my soul. My familiar sense of physical oneness with my bike extended outward, providing a visceral connection with the mountains around me, my fellow riders, the universe. In a way, this awe helped ground me, reminding me of my insignificance among greater forces while giving me a sense of meaning and purpose.

Still, I had to get this 170-pound body of mine across thirty miles of hill climbing at mile-high elevations. Biking had always been the strongest of my three triathlon sports, but it didn't make it easy.

The trick to a successful triathlon is to manage your energy expenditure. Energy can be measured objectively in watts or heart rate, or subjectively—just based on how you feel. Either way, you have to regulate your efforts. Whether you're feeling great or struggling to keep pace, you need to keep your level of exertion as constant as possible. On a scale of 1 to 10, if you can stay in the 6 to 7 range for the entire race, that's the sweet spot. I shoot for a five or six exertion level, enough for mortals like me to comfortably muddle through.

I completed the bike course just over my expected goal time, satisfied that I didn't struggle much climbing the hills. I felt energetic as I unclipped my bike shoes and headed into the transition area.

Feet on the Ground

The first big gut check in the race comes when my feet hit the ground off the bike leg. In either half or full-distance races, particularly on extremely hot, windy, or rainy days, there will be times when the body or mind starts sending warning signals.

When I get to T2, the transition from bike to run, I run a quick self-assessment. Are my legs cramping as I reach down to put on my running shoes? Are my feet too swollen from hours on hot pedals to properly lace up my running shoes? Am I shivering so much I want a blanket and a warm cup of soup? Throughout the course of my race history, I've answered "yes" to at least one of those questions at every single Ironman distance race—but I always managed to muddle through anyway. That's just part of the sport.

This time, I detected a problem as soon as I started to run; the inside of my left thigh felt wonky and sore. This was not a cramp or a pulled muscle because my gait remained steady, with no impingement or sharp pains. It's not a triathlon if you don't face some challenge or duress. Worst case scenario, I'd need to run through it or just walk the final miles. I have never had to abandon a race or walk over a finish line before. I would find my way that day.

In triathlons, just like with everyday life challenges, things have a way of working out—if you have patience and the confidence to persevere. I never felt great the first few miles of any run, so I knew to start slow, especially when recovering from a thirty-mile bike ride.

After averaging almost twelve minutes per mile for the first three miles, I found my groove. I ran the last three miles with a negative split, meaning that each mile went faster than the first three.

Crossing the finish line with my arms raised and trademark trot and grin, I felt ready to celebrate this personal victory. Anyone with the guts to show up and challenge themselves to overcome their doubts and limitations was a winner. I had raced in every type of triathlon in every conceivable condition. With nothing left to prove to myself or anyone else, I raced for pure joy—because I could.

I did not receive a participation medal or shiny prize for my race results that day. The best reward was waiting at the finish line. My daughter usually had enough time to eat lunch, change her clothes, and take a quick nap before I finished an Ironman distance race. In today's shorter-distance race, she still finished almost an hour before me. There she was, her face glowing. As I hugged my daughter, her ear-to-ear smile filled my whole, exhausted being with gratitude enough to sustain a lifetime of optimism. Some wonder why triathletes put themselves through such punishing training and racing conditions. *This* is why.

Copper Triangle

I don't always need the pomp, crowds, and thrills of official races. I derive so much pleasure just from riding my bike. One of my favorite rides in Colorado is the Copper Triangle—but it's a long, hilly, brutal ride.

In July, six months after my brain tumor surgery, I rode the route with Evan. Olympic triathlon and half-marathon notwithstanding, this was my longest ride and hardest effort since that Ironman race the September before.

The Copper Triangle is an iconic rocky mountain course covering over eighty miles and 6,000 vertical feet of mountain passes. The route describes a perfect triangle, starting at

Copper Mountain, climbing to Leadville and the Tennessee Pass, then descending into Minturn and Vail before one final epic climb up the Vail Pass. This challenging course combines the majesty of the Rocky Mountains with high country, great descents, panoramic views, and always some variable weather. Getting to ride this beloved route with my son once more meant the world to me.

As I watched Evan easily pass me up and climb ahead, I thought back to that first bike race he competed in at age twelve, joining his old man in the George Washington Bridge Challenge. Ever since that moment when he got up from his first crash and hopped right back on the bike, Evan was hooked. He went on to join the New York City junior racing program, which held events in the city's iconic Central Park. Even though Evan shifted to running after college, he and I will always treasure our shared love for biking. Doing this favorite ride together felt like a testament to that bond.

My thoughts continued to meander, much like the landscape around us. Next, they turned to the story and history of the famous 10th Mountain Division—which often came to mind when I rode this particular route.

The Tenth is a storied unit in the United States Army, renowned for its specialized training in mountain and winter warfare. They're best remembered for the Battle of Riva Ridge in the Apennine Mountain of Northern Italy, but their training was based in Camp Hale, outside Leadville, Colorado. On February 18, 1945, the Tenth Mountain Division successfully executed a night climb and surprise attack, overcoming German occupiers and securing a strategic victory that broke them into the Po Valley and led to the end of the fighting in Italy. This American division lost more troops than any other army unit in World War II.

As I drew close to Camp Hale, my thoughts began to oscillate between these courageous troops and my mother. Susan Cooper was only a child when these soldiers fought, but while she was a victim of Nazi terror, she was also a fighter—determined to not only survive but also to raise a son to thrive in this world.

Valor is a powerful word. For soldiers, it connotes courage and determination in the face of danger or difficulty. This same definition fits my mother.

It is impossible to live through a war unchanged, whether as a soldier, civilian, or refugee. In the Jewish tradition, there's a term for a woman of valor—*Eshet Chayil* in Hebrew. It describes a resourceful, compassionate, protective woman who evokes God's grace. My mother was such a woman.

The words *Eshet Chayil* are now inscribed on her gravestone. I'll never fully know who Susan Cooper was as a child before Hitler annexed Czechoslovakia in 1939 and the atrocities of war landed on her doorstep. But I know who she became: a resourceful, compassionate woman of valor.

This ride through the Copper Triangle began to feel like a timeless tribute to my family bonds, present, past, and future—both with my son, Evan, who took that ride with me that beautiful summer day and with my mother.

It took optimism for her and her five siblings to survive the Holocaust, and it will take optimism for me to continue living my life to its fullest despite my diagnosis. Like her, I've decided to anchor into my inner strength and focus on cultivating a legacy—for Evan and for all our kids, grandkids, and the generations to come—a legacy of leaving the world somehow, in some small way, *better*.

Until then, I'll focus on pure gratitude for every last moment I get.

Chapter 14
On Balance

February 3, 2024: After the fall

Triathlons can quickly become all-consuming. You start with a swimsuit, an old beater bike, and basic running shoes. *What could be easier than getting up in the morning for a quick jog, bike ride, or lap swim?*

Next, you start test-riding specialized trail bikes and ordering high-performance one-piece triathlon suits. Before you know it, you're researching coaches to help you make sense of the complexities of your training schedule.

By the time I got hooked on triathlons, I was also hitting my professional stride as a fintech founder and juggling the responsibilities of family life. Let's just say that once you exceed fifteen training hours per week—in addition to an entrepreneur's schedule—it's best to ensure that everyone's on board with your plan.

If I'm honest, it wasn't until recent years—following our 2017 move to Denver, Colorado—that I started to really get the hang of that elusive virtue: *balance*.

We moved to Denver for no better reason than it was time for a change. The air gets stale when you stay in one place too long. Neither of us wanted to live our entire lives within the island of Manhattan and the surrounding boroughs and suburbs, so we decided to trade skyscrapers and urban sprawl for Rocky Mountain views. Lucky for us, Jess also relocated to Denver, the very same summer we did—and Evan would join us within a few years, for the "good life" of outdoor sports.

When we moved, I was ready to put entrepreneurship behind me—to throw in the towel at the top of my game. In fact, I'd already landed a business development and sales position in Colorado. While Beth, now a newly retired high school math teacher, began building out her growing tutoring network, I hit the ground running.

My first job in Denver was with a Fortune 500 Payment Processing company—but after thirty-five years as a sales leader and a former founder, I quickly learned that that level of corporate bureaucracy and politics wasn't for me. So, I returned to the fintech world. Over the next few years, I'd work at various Colorado startups—as long as they followed my "Cooper Rules" and Criteria:

Would this job move me forward?
Would I have a seat at the table?

I needed to feel that I'd sooner regret *not* taking a job than taking it…Oh, and the last unwritten rule was: *I didn't work for assholes.*

Following these rules, I naturally accumulated a large network of colleagues, clients, associates, and friends. Not just through work, but also by volunteering, especially with immigrant populations and aspiring entrepreneurs. I got involved as a mentor with the local branch of the Founders Institute, a worldwide organization to help people in the early stages of launching a business.

I've always enjoyed helping people and connecting them with others to foster new relationships and opportunities. That said, it took me a long time to realize just how much the power of my network could also benefit me. I needed to first let go of the one thing still getting in my way. I had to learn to *relax*.

I began to notice how personally I took every sales rejection and—especially—every lack of response from a potential investor. I expected a *yes*. I could live with a *no* while demanding transparent, thorough feedback. But it infuriated me when prospects simply failed to respond.

If you've ever hit a baseball, you probably know that it's much easier to do if you don't grip the bat too tightly. I was starting to realize how excessively tight my grip on the bat had grown over the years and decades, both at work and in life.

It wasn't just pressure to win or succeed; I felt I had something to *prove*.

In baseball, when you grip the bat too tightly, it reduces your wrist flexibility and counterintuitively weakens the speed and power of your swing.

That said, grip too loose and you compromise impact force. Once again, it's all about balance. Get your grip right, and you'll gain the accuracy and force needed to hit that "sweet spot" on the ball.

Everything became easier when I loosened my grip. I closed more deals and wasted less time with bad prospects. I still had an edge and could push people and organizations too hard at times, but over the past few years, I had gotten better at finding the sweet spot.

So, what changed?

For one thing, I began to recognize the fulfillment I got out of helping people to level up. My big epiphany in business came when I realized that helping others achieve their goals and dreams, as long as they were aligned with mine—*that* was what really motivated me. So, I decided to invest more into that. In addition to my volunteer work with the Founders Institute, I enrolled in a 2020 training course to become a mindset coach.

Mindset Coach Training

The impulse that led me to sign up for coach training also prompted me to start the IronCEO blog and videos. I'd learned so much from my experiences, and I wanted to help others apply the same mental skills and key principles—to help them see results in their own lives.

In early fall, 2020, halfway through this training program, I joined an intensive workshop on Timeline therapy (TLT). This therapy deconstructs how attitudes and beliefs form within the unconscious mind, giving rise to conscious emotions and behaviors. It's designed to help people identify, explore, and heal the origins of impactful or traumatic events.

First, the practitioner helps you relax through deep breathing and guided meditation, similar to hypnosis. Then, you identify what limiting belief or negative emotion you want to release or change, as well as any patterns and events surrounding these beliefs and emotions.

The practitioner will ask, "Is this the earliest event where the negative belief or emotion occurred?" Eventually, once you dig all the way back in time to what feels like the original catalyst, you're asked to move to a place in your timeline where you no longer feel these negative emotions. Finally, you're guided to return to the source of the pain—in order to revise, release, and reframe the patterns with a new, positive lens.

When it 'came my turn to be a subject, I wanted to deconstruct my intense irritation when sales prospects either didn't return my messages or failed to disclose why they'd chosen a competitor's solution. It's not a big deal to have these feelings. Surely, every salesperson gets frustrated by their prospects. But for me, the emotions led to unproductive and unhealthy behaviors. I would push potential customers away by revealing my frustration. I knew I might still have won their business if I'd acted differently. Either way, I'd be better off using my energy on new opportunities—if I could just *let things go*.

During my TLT-guided meditation, I was surprised by how far back in my timeline these work-related frustrations went. I followed that chip on my shoulder back all the way through my earliest days.

In fact, this defense mechanism seemed to predate my own birth, reaching back into my generational bloodline. It first showed up to protect me from the whispers and taboos surrounding my mother's trauma and the outsider feeling that accompanied me to school and synagogue. I knew I was loved and provided for, but my early solitude and fraught silence taught me I'd have to protect and fend for myself.

Weight of the Past

After two mentally exhausting days on Zoom training calls, studying, and practicing TLT, I needed a break and a fresh perspective. So, I did what I always do when it's time to recharge. I went for a bike ride.

Since we were back in New Jersey for my stepdaughter Molly's wedding, I picked one of my favorite old area routes. It meandered some forty miles past the densely packed Northern New Jersey suburbs and into the serene, rustic roads of New York's southern Rockland County.

I watched golden leaves shimmering on the trees and breathed the crisp air as I hit the cycling super highway known as 9W. I'd biked this route countless times with various riding groups. Today, I was solo, exactly what I needed to absorb the teachings of the last two days.

Then—like a crack of thunder—a weighty revelation jostled me from my biking meditation. I remember the exact spot where it happened: along the winding, bumpy South Mountain Road. As I pedaled furiously to maintain speed and momentum, I found myself reliving the swirl of emotions from my TLT practice session.

Suddenly, I could see my patterns from a broader vantage point, including my belief that, without a father, siblings, or close extended family, I would always have to go it alone.

At that moment on my bike, I also saw the extent to which I treated ordinary events as matters of life or death. If you didn't agree with me, you were *against* me, or else blocking me from moving forward—not just to get what I wanted to advance, but to get what I thought I needed, *to survive.*

This, more than any ADHD diagnosis, explained my primal need for forward momentum. Staying in motion felt elemental to my very being. Just as my ancestors constantly moved to stay warm, find food, and decide their next moves, stagnation always registered with me as some sort of mortal threat.

The very next moment, a weight seemed to lift. It dawned on me that I could no longer feel that chip I'd carried on my shoulder my whole life.

While my survivor heritage is still a part of me, I no longer wear that label as some heavy burden or shield. Better to say that I've tucked those inherited instincts away in a safe place. These days, I try to only bring them out when they're actually needed.

I'll always be proud of the strength my mother passed down to me. But I've also learned to release the heavy pain surrounding that label and reframe it as resilience, determination, and independence. As I climbed those hilly roads, my body and soul grounded into the belief that I could not just endure, but also open to and grow from every one of life's experiences—including perceived failures and even rejections.

I had both survived and succeeded, and nobody could take it away. For the first time, I felt free. Released from my expectations and unquenched desire to "show the world" what I was made of.

I had nothing left to prove.

Retirement

At the time, I had no idea that in just a few years, I'd receive a brain cancer diagnosis, forcing me to retire from full-time work. Before that revelation on my bike, retirement might have felt like deadly stagnation. Now it felt like more of a concept than a reality. I certainly didn't mind stepping away from the daily grind of deals, commissions, and sales quotas—to turn my sights toward new horizons. New starting lines.

With or without cancer, I had hit the cusp of my so-called "golden years." Upon moving to Colorado, I befriended retirees who seemed content with their new lifestyle—as well as those who resisted the change, either due to an enduring passion for their field or simply because they lacked meaningful hobbies and interests outside of work.

Luckily, I've never been afraid to reinvent myself, and I have plenty of personal and business projects to keep me busy. In addition to my ongoing—if substantially revised—fitness regimen (and writing this book), I serve on the board of a Colorado startup founded by a Nigerian immigrant living in Denver. I helped them build a payments and remittance platform to serve African diaspora communities and businesses abroad that require dollars to pay their foreign suppliers. As a first-generation American, I know the struggles and challenges for immigrants and the positive impact they make on society through elbow grease and a desire to forge a better life.

I also have a loving wife and a growing family—especially since both Jess and Evan followed our lead, relocating to

Colorado. Jess and her husband, Mike, moved to Denver the same summer as us. As I write this, they're expecting their first child in just a few months—due in May 2024. Evan, now in his early thirties, also moved to Colorado for the "good life" of cycling, skiing, and running.

Cancer may have forced me to leave my full-time career behind, but retirement helped test my newfound ability to loosen my grip and really focus on the impact of my actions—on serving others in a more direct way. I've learned that true resilience doesn't contract or control; it comes from meeting challenges with inner flexibility.

Entrepreneurs are a different breed in many respects. We tend to see problems and needs that others miss, then convince ourselves we're uniquely qualified to solve them. Founders often have that survivor or outsider edge because we need grit and determination to overcome the heavy obstacles of starting a business.

That said, let's bust the myth of entrepreneurs as risk-taking, swashbuckling heroes only out for the big payday. Starting any business may involve risks—but most successful entrepreneurs are *risk mitigators*, not risk takers. The idea is to reduce risk through expertise, customer and market research, and constantly testing your own assumptions.

Growing up, my favorite Mets player was Bud Harrelson. He was a light-hitting shortstop with a great glove and a fiery attitude. You could count on Buddy to make contact at the plate and score his share of singles and doubles.

Like Bud Harrelson, I never swung for the fences—and that's okay. Going three for three by selling each one of my start-ups marks a solid life's work. As they say in baseball, you are the back of your baseball card. My statistics show that, while I wasn't willing to take on huge risks, I could consistently hit for average.

I may not rank among the Entrepreneur's Hall of Fame, but these days, the only personal stats I revel in come in the form of miles. According to my fitness app, I've reached over 6,000 miles of swimming, biking, running, hiking, and skiing in recent years alone. While I may not be the best of the best, those are numerical accomplishments I can feel proud of.

Second Surgery

In late November 2023, my oncologist informed us that new cancer cells had appeared next to the original resection. Given my continued strength and relative health, the doctors recommended another surgery as the best, most aggressive option. Once again, we scheduled a brain surgery, this time on December 11, 2023.

As Yogi Berra once said, "It's *deja vu* all over again." But, as I prepared for the surgery, I realized that each experience in our lives is unique. This time I knew how expectations could soon become New York City-sized potholes, so I tried to stay grounded and realistic.

While Beth assured me that the surgeon gave the exact same speech about risks, dangers, and outcomes as before—for some reason, it landed differently. I still hoped for similar results, but this time I felt more vulnerable and more conscious of the risks—at least until I talked things over with my radiologist, whom I considered my confidante, fellow triathlete, and friend.

Just like the previous January, I agreed to stay awake during critical moments of the surgery. The surgeon again successfully removed most of the tumor cells and avoided any areas that would unnecessarily harm my cognitive or sensory capabilities. This second surgery only took three hours, and while I remember being awake, the whole thing seemed faster, easier, and less stressful.

Even the recovery went more smoothly. Within a matter of weeks, I was already planning a ski trip to one of my favorite spots on earth: Jackson Hole Mountain Resort in Teton Village, Wyoming.

I never expected that, in less than two months, I'd be right back on the operating table. This time not because of cancer, but because of my own lingering struggles to maintain balance—both metaphorically and also in a very literal way.

Jackson Hole Mountain Resort

I can't honestly say I ever got a "green light" from anyone to go skiing, not after the first surgery or the second. My doctors clearly didn't love the idea, and Beth mainly just knew she couldn't stop me, so everyone decided the best approach would be to ensure that I took it slow and had supervision.

That was fine with me. This was no longer about some chip on my shoulder that kept me compulsively moving forward—nor even about the thrill of a swift descent through the snow. This time, it mainly had to do with the pull of the natural landscape. Jackson Hole Mountain Resort has come to feel like my spiritual center. The older I get, the more my soul feels intertwined within those majestic peaks and valleys.

So, on February 1, 2024, I flew out to Jackson with my friend Gary, and my son Evan. The ski resort is named for the valley formed by the Gros Ventre and Teton ranges. It nestles among the glaciers, lakes, and grazing wild elk of the Grand Teton and Yellowstone National Parks. Plus, it's near one of my favorite watering holes, the Million Dollar Cowboy Bar, featuring saddle-like bar stools and elk antlers at every corner.

A few days before this trip, back in Colorado, I skied a little to prepare and take stock of my abilities. I noticed the same coordination issues with right-side deficits, so I knew I'd have to be mindful and adapt to my limitations.

Once we made it to the resort, we passed by the Jackson Hole aerial tram, and I noticed their iconic sign. Here's what it said:

SAFETY MESSAGE

Our mountain is like nothing you have skied before! It is huge, with variable terrain from groomed slopes to dangerous cliff areas and dangerously variable weather and snow conditions. You must always exercise extreme caution. You could become lost. You could make a mistake and suffer personal injury or death. Protect yourself— understand the trail map and ask questions before you ski. Obey all trail signs and markers. Please think and be careful.
Show this special mountain the respect it demands.

Fair enough, I thought. I'll start slow and "exercise extreme caution."

"You guys go and take the first run up the tram," I said. "I'll just walk around the base and loosen up."

The Fall

After about an hour, Evan and Gary returned, and I got ready for my first run. I chose to take a very easy route up the mountain. Still, after only 30 yards or so, I took a mild spill. It was a pretty insignificant fall, and I was able to get right back up with Evan's assistance.

Then, not two hundred yards later, I once again lost all equilibrium and body control. With no warning and quick as a whip, I fell backward. This time, I landed full force on the back of my head—right next to the incision sites for both my surgeries.

The impact knocked me out cold for a few minutes, but Evan was there in a flash. Within a few minutes, medical personnel and ski patrol were wrapping me in a blanketed cocoon and loading me onto a medical sled.

After a brief check-up at the resort's medical station, an ambulance took me to the nearest emergency room, about a twenty-minute drive from the mountain. They ran some preliminary tests before sending me back to our hotel room in Jackson. The whole thing felt utterly surreal, as I'd never taken a serious fall or sustained a major accident despite my decades of adrenaline-chasing activities.

It wasn't until the next morning that we realized I wasn't yet out of the woods—not by a long shot.

Surprise Surgery

When I called my neurologist back home in Denver, the team made one thing very clear: I had to get back to the hospital ASAP for an emergency MRI to see what else might be going on in my brain.

So, on the second day of our ski trip, Evan and I returned bright and early to the local hospital for the scan. That's when we realized I had a hematoma—serious internal bleeding—at the back of my skull.

This needed to be dealt with—STAT—by a neurosurgeon.

In the dark of night, I was put on a medical plane at Jackson's local airport to fly to a facility in eastern Idaho, where they prepared to perform my surgery the very next day: Saturday, February 3, 2024.

For this operation, I would not have the benefit of weeks of preparation, nor certainly, the option to stay awake and calmly answer questions. They had to immediately treat the hematoma by making an incision to drain internal bleeding. Otherwise, the pressure would continue to build up, possibly resulting in major brain damage, a hemorrhagic stroke, or even death.

During the surgery, they found and also removed a potentially dangerous build-up of dried blood from my previous operation. Within thirty minutes, the procedure was done, Evan and Beth were at my bedside. Beth flew out to meet us, having cut short her family visit in Florida, she hopped on the earliest flight she could find.

Aftermath

Like most things, the impact of this unexpected third brain surgery didn't sink in right away. I may have carried a chip on my shoulder for most of my life, but I've never been an alarmist. In fact, I often err on the side of optimism, underestimating just how bad things can get.

But waking from that surgery to find I could no longer move my right side nearly *at all*—I knew my life was taking a new course.

There's a fine line sometimes between optimism and outright denial. I wanted to stay on the realistic side of that line. While I knew I would not be this limited forever, the fact remained that just two days before, I'd felt ready to ski down snowy mountainsides—and now I suddenly couldn't get out of bed, nor even go to the bathroom without help.

For about a week, I remained in that Idaho hospital, working on physical therapy exercises, mainly to ensure I could walk out of there on my own two feet and get up and down a flight of stairs.

Early the morning of Friday, February 9th, we got approvals and paperwork for my release and drove the 10 hours to Denver—but instead of settling in at home, I checked into a nearby rehabilitation center, where I'd stay for the next two weeks. My chances for recovery were uncertain, so I settled into the knowledge that my life might be seriously and permanently altered.

Balance and Acceptance

There's a lot I can say about the concept of balance. One thing I know is that balance is not some midpoint, with 50 percent on one side and an equal 50 percent on the other. Instead, think of it as an equilibrium. The balancing point shifts based on your priorities at specific points in your life.

While I consider myself a lifelong athlete, there have been extended periods where my overall fitness was not a priority. Life certainly gets in the way sometimes. Starting a family while building a successful business can consume your time and energy, and it's easy to find excuses to not exercise.

We all find ways to prioritize what's important to us, but not all of us will find balance. And while it may have taken me longer than some, I eventually succeeded in building my life around the activities, responsibilities, and above all, the people that matter most.

I was grateful for that fact as I muddled through my physical therapy back in Denver. Ironman competitions and high-risk skiing may have been over, but I still appreciated the good people around me and had plenty to look forward to.

During this time, I slowly recovered most—but not all—of my previous mobility and coordination. Still, my speech remained a bit slurred at times and some cognitive abilities (mental calculations, spelling, keeping track of time) felt difficult and slow.

Unlike my earlier response when sales prospects ghosted me, I did not allow myself to get overwhelmed by frustration. All told, it didn't take me too long to accept my new reality. Maybe I got that from my mother, another benefit from the old survival DNA.

I could almost hear Mom saying it: *what choice did I have?*

I knew I'd created this reality for myself. There was no one else to blame. Just like the ominous tram sign at the Jackson

Hole Ski Resort had tried to warn me, I was knowingly taking on a big risk.

Do I wish that the accident hadn't occurred or that I'd taken more precautions? Sure. I would have less to deal with now. But while I can accept responsibility for what I put myself and my family through, I'm not wallowing in regret.

Nor has anyone who knows me expressed much shock. One friend even chuckled and said, "We fully expected some blaze of glory from you!"

Whether at Jackson Hole or closer to home, I had always done what I had resolved to do, from running my first triathlon to competing in my 10th Ironman race, and everything in between—even if it meant getting a bit obsessed with my fitness goals for a decade or five.

I'm not trying to congratulate myself on taking undue risks or stubbornly doing things my way. But at this point, I know who I am.

As I mentioned earlier, the entrepreneur mindset may be prone to extremes, but we also don't scare easy. When you're a founder, everyone loves to point out the fact that nine out of ten startups fail. There's this sense that you have to be bold. You have to accept risks. But you'd be wise to also accept that no one's entitled to success—even if, like me, you don't really consider failure to be an option.

Likewise, every endurance athlete realizes they're not entitled to cross that finish line. You have to put in the work, accept all the variables involved, keep moving forward, and above all, keep showing up at the starting line.

I always ran my own calculus when it came to risk assessment. Early in my life and career, I couldn't really afford the risk of failure, so I always felt I was taking *acceptable* risks. Like Bud Harrelson, I wanted a prominent—not an overly risky or even necessarily spectacular—career. Of course, it's all relative. But that's how I looked at it.

Even when it came to hitting the slopes of Jackson Hole a few months after my second brain cancer surgery, I was still—in my view—staying within the margins of acceptable risk. That may sound a bit crazy to some. But (until that last miscalculation), I'd always had a pretty good sense of my physical limitations. More to the point: to me, being afraid to live my life or take any chances—that was the bigger risk. I never wanted to go in that direction. Much like my rules for choosing a job, I was more afraid of regretting the things I never did.

By March 2024, my medical team confirmed some difficult news: my tumor had been spreading again. They explained that if I hadn't taken such a major fall, I might be a little bit better off right now—but not all my deficits could be explained by the ski accident.

This was going to happen anyway.

While I didn't expect these new limitations—or at least not so soon—the experience has provided me with a new challenge and a new realization. The real trick to balance lies tucked into that simple yet powerful adage: "Change what you can, accept what you can't, and figure out the difference."

Anytime you lose your equilibrium and take a big fall, you have the same choice. You can smash your fists against the wall in pointless resistance. Or you can gracefully accept what's out of your hands—then get busy focusing on what matters.

Chapter 15
Core of the IronCEO

April 22, 2024: Passover Seder

Needless to say, I've had to adjust my daily routine away from swimming, biking, and running. These days you might find me sitting in my wheelchair, but I don't consider myself "disabled" for a minute. I assure you I'm still the same person, and I still put in the work with mobility and bodyweight exercises every single day.

Does this mean the IronCEO has met his match with cancer?

Not the way I see it.

Iron sounds like an indestructible element—and yes, the triumph of crossing that particular finish line and hearing those words—"You are an IRONMAN!"—does build enormous confidence. But also? Anyone who has earned that title understands just how vulnerable, how *human*, they really are.

I may have completed ten Ironman races, but everything's relative. In my case, it's "relative" in more ways than one, given that my son and daughter have outperformed my racing stats at every turn (and I couldn't be prouder).

The loss of my ability to train and race certainly put my IronCEO Mindset to the test. How do I live life to its fullest when deprived of the goals and practices that formed so much of my identity?

The answer is: I dig deeper.

I'll admit that I don't always like what I find. As you can imagine, there's plenty of fear and discomfort involved in living with cancer. But I've also found that when I can truly accept the things out of my control and appreciate the gifts I still have, I'm amazed by how much meaning there is to find.

Birthday Celebrations

My goal now is to spend as much time as I can, focused on what I can do every day to enjoy life. I'd say I succeed with this at least 80 percent of the time. Now and then, I get an amazing gift of a day fully at peace and cherish each moment. That surprise Bruce Springsteen concert definitely made the cut. So did my most recent birthday celebrations.

The day before my 62nd birthday, I received a surprise visitor: my childhood friend, Steve! He flew into Denver that Sunday afternoon and took Beth and me out for a fantastic sushi dinner. I even indulged in a little illicit saké (in defiance of my doctor's recommendations). The next day, I reveled in the best company possible: my loving wife and kids.

At temple the following Saturday, our rabbi asked me to come up for an *aliyah* in honor of my birthday. This Hebrew term means "going up," which refers to both ascending to the platform called the *bimah* and to a spiritual ascent. To receive this sacred rite, you have to be of bar mitzvah age—which is when I did my first one.

Rabbi Korbin gifted me with the first of the seven aliyahs scheduled for that service. I deeply appreciated both this position of honor and this new, young Rabbi, whose *derashot* (homilies) struck me as relatable and insightful. As I sat in front of the congregation in my wheelchair, I realized that nearly fifty years had passed since the first time I nervously rose to this occasion.

That's when Rabbi Korbin got down on one knee to meet my eye level, and said the following words:

"Alex, you've long shown us all the meaning of words like *resilience* and *fortitude* through your decades of endurance racing, all while building a successful career and a beautiful family. Not everyone can pursue personal goals with such commitment and strength, but what impresses me most of all is how you make people feel, through your sincerity, sense of humor, and the faithful dedication you show to everyone you love."

It's moments like these when I realize that the greatest sin is taking your life for granted. I know more than anyone else how often I've taken the wrong tact or turn (especially given my compulsive need to keep moving). But looking back, I'm happy to at least say that while I may have tried to squeeze a bit too much into the average day—and ended up too often running late to engagements as a result—I did try to do right by my people: my mother, my friends, and my family.

Faith and Affiliation

To be honest, I've gone to temple only occasionally since my diagnosis. I ended my official affiliation with my previous synagogue more than ten years ago upon becoming deeply ambivalent about organized religions in general.

I remain spiritually curious, recently exploring modern reinterpretations of ancient traditions like Buddhism, Hinduism, Taoism, and Stoicism. Not because I'm looking to convert, though. Like many "cultural Jews," I feel deeply connected to my ancestry.

I was born a Jew, and I will die as a Jew, with a proper Jewish burial. That is the least I can do to honor my father and mother and the Jewish heritage that condemned much of our family to death at the hands of the Nazis.

My mother never discussed her feelings about God or religion. I wouldn't blame her for being angry with God or losing her faith altogether. (Maybe that's why I couldn't bring myself to ask.) It's hard to imagine how a God who created and loves humanity would allow such terrible things to occur.

Likewise, I could place the blame for my cancer—and the cancers that took both my parents—on some divine force, but I don't. Nor do I expect some loving deity to intervene and save me from my fate. It's just the genes I got.

That said, I also acknowledge that sometimes, either the coincidences feel a bit too great or the blessings a bit too lavish to not at least allow in some room for faith in...something bigger.

I may lack the words or certainty to describe or persuade anyone, but I do sense there's some powerful force at play here in life. That we are all connected by something greater tying us together, whether atoms or energies or interconnected souls. Most of all, I believe that how we impact and honor those connections deeply matters.

Athletes and business owners like to say, "There's no such thing as luck," but I consider myself deeply fortunate in many ways. Given that both my parents survived World War II concentration camps, I'm happy to even be here at all. I certainly lucked out with the mother I got—an amazing survivor, provider, and true woman of valor—as well as the beautiful family I've raised.

Above all, I've learned to cherish that precious human asset: *time*. I know plenty of people diagnosed with cancer who died within a few months. They hardly had time to face this new reality, put their affairs in order, and say their goodbyes. On the other hand, I've been given ample opportunity to reflect and prepare. Sometimes I wonder *why*.

Not just: *Why was I given this time?* But also: *Why* this *cancer?* Glioblastomas affect only several thousand people a year, and the prognosis is invariably grave.

While that's obviously a short straw, this cancer—*my* specific, individual cancer—also allowed me to live with almost no side effects or impairments for more than a year. During that time, I got to exercise daily, race triathlons and half-marathons, and take trips with my wife. For all intents and purposes, I was the same spirited husband, father, grandfather, and friend as always. My weight and looks barely changed—especially considering I had no hair to lose in the first place.

I called it my "cheap parlor trick," but of course, I wasn't trying to trick anyone and there was no magic involved—just hard work, a good attitude, and what I can only explain as either "angels from above" or good, old-fashioned luck of the draw.

Either way, I'm grateful I got this chance to put my IronCEO Mindset to the ultimate test. At the end of the day, it's not so much what happens to you but the beliefs and interpretations you apply to your life and the meaning you choose to make out of it all.

The antidote to morbid prognostication is to live life to its fullest. Thanks to my family history, I'm an old hand at viewing every day as if it's my last. I was bequeathed this inheritance when my father died three months after I was born and my mother died two days after my 38th birthday. I hope to pass this, my most valuable legacy, onto my wife, children, and grandchildren.

Passover

A few weeks after my birthday, Beth and I prepared to host the Passover Seder, an occasion to gather over a deeply symbolic and delicious meal.

This year's table was bigger than ever, with the third generation making their appearance in the form of our granddaughters, Noa (Ben's four-year-old) and Ella (Molly's nine-month-old)—and yet another soon-to-make his-or-her big debut. For the occasion, Jess was more than eight months into her pregnancy, looking radiant and excited for the upcoming life transformation.

I was thrilled to invite our Israeli son-in-law, Tomer (Molly's husband) to co-officiate this year. He blessed us with his fluent Hebrew, while I added the storytelling flourish. I've always enjoyed this aspect of the Seder: sharing stories and histories that honor our shared cultural past.

This year, my past came to mind. As an only child, I'd grown up thinking of myself as some kind of lone wolf. I gravitated toward individual sports, starting my own things, and doing them my own way.

Looking around, it occurred to me that I never really expected to have so much family. Not that I'd planned to live some hermetic, solitary existence. I've always been outgoing, and I tend to make friends everywhere I go. In fact, I also made my own family, not just by blending two homes—Beth's and my own—into something greater and stronger, but also in terms of feeling deeply connected to a community or group of friends.

Looking around that Seder table and seeing the big family my wife and I built, I felt a surge of pride and gratitude. The family, the community, the network—all the connections form part of our respective journeys. Building connections that matter, no matter how you do it, that's something to be proud of. At that moment, I recalled my personal work in delving deep into my ancestral line to heal old hurts and unravel some of my egoic knots. Now here I was sitting at the head of a table of three generations.

I'm all for personal achievements. They can fuel you to get out there and do something with your life. It's great to build a solid, meaningful career, provide for those you love, and do things you're passionate about. But I'll say one thing: I could dump out all the boxes of medals from all the races I've done because not one of those shiny accolades matters to me.

The main question for me is this: *How did I impact those around me? Did I make things better while I was here, for myself and for others?*

These are the real essentials.

To Be Loved

Neither slogans nor battle cries will save me from the fate of my cancer. But my passion for life delivers what I need. While I still could, I filled my calendar with races and vacations to restore a sense of normalcy.

Now that I've had to slow down, I'm glad for my ability to accept things as they are—but that doesn't mean I don't struggle at times. This path is harder than any race course I've encountered. It's painful to see those I've always taken care of and provided for—especially Beth—needing to step in and care for me.

I don't want to appear pollyannaish, but my new life has also brought some benefits. My love for Beth and my appreciation for our family has never been stronger. I've been humbled by the love and acts of kindness from family, friends, caregivers, and even strangers.

To better cultivate these moments of warmth, Beth, my beautiful, courageous, compassionate wife, started a new tradition for us shortly after my cancer diagnosis. Every evening, with few exceptions, after we finished dinner—before going upstairs to relax—we danced.

She and I took turns choosing a song for the night, then we took each other in our arms and danced in the living room. There's no denying that life is bittersweet, but when Beth and I danced, love was the only emotion coursing through me. The song that best expresses what I mean was made famous by Marvin Gaye and James Taylor: "How Sweet It Is (To Be Loved by You)."

The songs we danced to were usually about love, and we tried not to repeat the same one, but otherwise, there were no rules. We've let loose to rock songs. Other nights, we'd choose a soft sweet ballad, better suited to slower steps and a closer embrace.

Afterward, Beth meticulously recorded the song's name in a notebook with her practiced teacher's penmanship. Those pages tell a story of our love and life together as eloquent and meaningful as anything I've written here.

The "Big Finish"

In every single race I've ever swum, biked, and/or run, I have followed a personal rule. No matter how exhausted I feel, or how much pain I've endured, I always make sure to give my loved ones (and everyone else gathered at the line) a joyful *big finish*.

The ritual goes as follows: Beth meets me before I enter the finish line chute, collects unnecessary gear and layers, and energizes me with a kiss. Then, I gallop on, raising both my hands and flashing my signature IronCEO smile as I take those final, triumphant steps across the finish line.

I may have lost some of my strength and endurance, but I am not done yet.

I'm just beginning to stretch the boundaries of my resilience. Every day I have the choice of what to focus on. I could tell myself that this wasn't supposed to be my story. I could resist and shout and shake my fists at the sky, but then I wouldn't be in the moment. I wouldn't be living my life to its fullest, nor learning a damn thing from it.

That's not to say I never focus on the terminal nature of my diagnosis. Beth and I both think about it every day. But those thoughts don't weigh me down like an anchor. Rather, they tend to pass overhead like dark clouds over an otherwise clear day. The shadows they cast are just a part of living with cancer.

Everyone will get knocked down and suffer anguish and disappointment. Over the years, I've gathered the inner resources needed to overcome setbacks and climb back on the bike when I fall. But while mindset will not defeat my cancer, it does give me the strength and grace to carry on and live my best life.

In Queens, I learned to ride a bike, properly hit a baseball, and improvise side hustles.

In college, I applied my passion for starting new things to help found Vassar's inaugural men's baseball team and earn a degree in the then-brand-new field of cognitive science.

Finally, as a New Jersey entrepreneur (and latter-day Coloradoan), I built a family, launched three businesses, and developed my thirst for competition into decades of triathlons and ten Ironman races.

I never expected to get sucked into the endurance life back in Northern New Jersey when I signed up for the Road Dawgs and GWB Challenge races. I was just looking for exercise, companionship, and some friendly competition. I couldn't be happier or more grateful for the lifetime of racing that followed.

These days, my sudden, unprecedented downtime has provided me the luxury of a deeper level of awareness and a regular meditation practice. I now understand a little more that "I" am not those wins I've achieved or any of the things I've done or do. Nor am I the words I write or the list of mindset principles I share with others.

Essentially, I'm not some identity I've consciously constructed or even my conscious mind itself, but rather something deeper, something inside of that. I want to understand the nature of that "something inside," which some might call a soul—and to be good with whatever I find there. Because in the end, that's what we're left with.

That, and the impact we leave behind.

In Ironman, as in many aspects of life, a finish is a huge win. But, as I said from the start, the finish happens naturally—if you can get there in the first place and keep going long enough.

Endings are inevitable, even when they're not the kind you want. But showing up in the first place? That's optional. You could sit out your whole life if you're not careful.

Of course, there's a lot to be said about big finishes, whether they come in the form of glory or sacrifice. But I'm not going to presume that my finish needs to be glorious or that it represents some noble sacrifice.

I'm more interested in how I've lived. To me, the true glory lies in just starting something and seeing where it takes me. I have never met anyone who ended up exactly where they planned to go in life. Unexpected twists and turns always crop up. What matters is what you get out of it, and sometimes it's best to not plan too much—to let the journey take you along.

As I said on the day of my last Ironman race: we never know what day we'll have triumph. We also never know which day will be our last. We're all guilty at times of moving too fast or not taking the time to examine or appreciate what we have. But it's showing up, more than anything else, that determines our life's path and legacy.

I didn't write this book to show everyone how great I am. I'm just here to look at it all—the good and bad alike—and hopefully find some meaning in it all. To me, *meaning* is not some fixed and settled conclusion. It's a continual journey of discovery, one I'm still trying to figure out.

I said at the start of my final Ironman race on September 11, 2002, that "sometimes, our destiny chooses us."

Meanwhile, the best we can do is maintain a grateful heart—and always have the courage to start what we will finish.

Epilogue

I had been thinking about writing my memoir for years before I got my cancer diagnosis. I wanted to share the benefits of what I called my "IronCEO Mindset," structured according to seven key principles that helped transform this immigrant's son from Queens into a three-time founder and ten-time Ironman:

1. Live life to its fullest.
2. Keep moving. (a.k.a. the "Cooper Rule")
3. Own the narrative.
4. Stay in the moment.
5. Develop resilience.
6. Be consistent.
7. Build confidence. (i.e. "Everything you have done has led to this moment.")

After my cancer diagnosis in late 2022, I naively believed that the story of my memoir would remain the same—I'd just add a chapter or two about the illness. But when I began writing, I soon realized I was no longer the same man. Both my life and my story have changed dramatically and continue to do so.

I'll always be the IronCEO, but I can no longer neatly package up my life's story under that title alone. I have followed the principles listed above and paid homage to them throughout the book. Because of them, I could more easily adapt to my cancer diagnosis and stay committed to meaningful goals—like continuing to train like an animal and even *race*, despite my first rounds of chemo and radiation treatments...until, of course, I couldn't.

While writing this book over the past year and some change, my mindset has evolved. I've had more time to reflect on themes of *survivorship*, *endurance*, and the nature of both *success* and *failure*, plus my commitment to *starting things from scratch* and my habit of *standing my ground*, especially in business. To me, that's a huge part of the path: being willing to take in new material. To dig deeper. To challenge your assumptions and release preconceptions.

Above all, this experience with cancer helped me find deeper meaning through the connections I've made in this human journey, as well as the unexpected—and unwelcome—life events I've faced.

In the end, I decided to add three more core "key principles" to my IronCEO Mindset:

8. Cultivate gratitude.
9. Find balance.
10. Make meaning.

We're all raised with different morals and models of how to be and how to live, but as I see it, it's on each one of us to determine our own individual mindset. To make meaning out of our lives, no matter the playing field or the hand we've been dealt, and to encourage others along the way.

I'd like to think that, while this book may have changed from the original vision I had in mind, it now reflects a more mature and balanced version of my IronCEO Mindset, one that still delights in pushing past limits, but also understands on a deeper level how to appreciate every moment of life—beyond just the cinematic glories and sacrifices.

I hold these IronCEO Mindset principles dear because they have allowed me to live life on my terms and get the most out of my years. I may never show up at the starting line of another Ironman race, but I *can* pay it forward by sharing the wealth with others. If even one of the principles hits home and helps you in some small way, I will have achieved my goal.

About the Author

Alex Cooper is a fintech innovator, business development dynamo, entrepreneur, Ironman competitor, and mindset coach.

From humble beginnings as an immigrant's son from Queens, Cooper went on to found three technology start-ups, two of which achieved Inc. 500 status and were sold to public companies. He also completed 10 Ironman competitions and countless other endurance races.

Cooper's proudest achievements, by far, include building a beautiful family with his loving wife, Beth, and helping other people make their dreams become reality through his IronCEO mindset principles.

Made in United States
North Haven, CT
23 June 2024

53985476R00143